The Modern Drama

*

A Play in Five Acts

*

Traumear

The Figures (or Players)

The preamble:

Two Gentlemen
A Superintendent of Police
A Policeman

Acts I - V

Trevor – the director of the drama
Alphonse – husband of Trish
Trish – wife of Alphonse
Miriam – natural mother of Tim
Galina – a woman
Vivian Clough – friend of Uncle Werner
Uncle Werner – a friend
Tim – son of Miriam,
        – adopted son of Alphonse and Trish

A Member of the Audience

The six members of the Chorus
    Ted – M1
    Carl – M2
    Frank – M3 – three young men or 3 males
    Lorraine – F1
    Annie – F2
    Rita – F3 – three young women or 3 females

Epilogue

Two Ladies of Leisure

---

iii

Index

*

The Modern Drama

(a Play in Five Acts)

Preamble,

(in three scenes)

Scene 1

(two Gentlemen)

GENT.1   There you are. And a good day to you.
Hope you weren't busy?

GENT.2   Never too busy to see you, my friend.
After all, what could be going on that
Would be more important?
Was it a little chat you wanted?
Or maybe a lengthy analysis of the day's problems?

GENT.1   Nothing so definite, I'm afraid.
A mere recognition of the fact
That nothing much is happening
And how this is dangerous.

GENT 2:   Oh come along! How, dangerous?
I thought we had it all figured out.

GENT.1   I thought so too.
And then I thought: my God,
that is a dangerous thought!
The last time I thought that,
Some years ago, the sky fell down.

GENT.2   Have I seen that coat on you before?
It's very nice. You always dress well.
If we keep up with the latest dress code,
What could go wrong in our lives?
That is what I tell Abigail.
And she believes me.

1

I like to know that her mind is concentrated
On one or two essentials.
It keeps the anxiety at bay.

GENT.1   I have no use for anxiety.
In fact I get anxious when I think about it.
I wish you hadn't mentioned it.
It will take me a while now to relax.
It's like a spook, is anxiety.

GENT.2   You may be on your way to a break-down,
Have you thought of that?
Or maybe a religious experience.
I suggest you welcome it with heart and soul.
Bring your emotion to the bar of justice.

GENT 1:   So how's it going, with you and Abigail?

GENT.2   Oh never ask that. Not directly like that.
Slide in on it from the side, if you like,
A comment like: Is Abigail well?
Or a complete lie like: Abigail is off to
London next week, isn't she? –
Even though you know fine well she isn't.
That gives me wriggle-room, don't you see.

GENT.1   Ho-hum. I'm not myself these days.
Not at home in my skin, if you know what I mean.
And then I wonder, should a man both healthy
And sane even think about that?

GENT.2   Not at all! Not at all! Get on to the next
Thing, don't you see. Notice and pass over.
Notice again … pass over again.
I make a good habit of that.
Never pay any attention to the psyche.
The psyche is a spoiled brat,
Deserves to be studiously ignored.

	Have you had lunch?
GENT.1	Of course. I mean no, not yet.
	But I don't want to have lunch now.
	I was hoping we would be able to speak like friends,
	Of this and that, including what bothers me.
GENT.2	But we are doing that, good grief!
	It's what we've been doing since we met.
	But you won't take my advice.
	You keep niggling and pestering.
	You are knocking your head against a wall.
	Very firmly tell yourself: I am happy!
	Then confirm that, maybe by
	Banging your fist against some hard object.
	Like this: I am happy! It never fails. Honestly.
	Modern man has to fight for his humanity.
	We are not born with our humanity firmly in
	Place, don't you know. We are surrounded by
	Nothing but dangers, risks and challenges …
GENT.1	To our humanity? That's a new one on me.
GENT.2	You better believe it. Tiresome but true.
	And your psyche is the trouble-maker.
	A lot of people realize that, nowadays,
	Which is why they hire their personal psychiatrist.
	They pay him to do the work.
	Of course you have to have money.
	Without money you're buggered.

(his telephone rings)

Wait, that's my phone. 'Hello?
Yes dear. Of course dear. If you like.
No, as it happens I'm not busy at all.
Fine. In ten minutes. See you there.'
Sorry about that. Abigail. Says it's urgent.
You'll keep in mind now what I said.

3

That really is a lovely Jacket.

*(**Gent. 2** leaves)*

GENT.1   Blablablablabla!
          As usual, talking gets me nowhere.
          And as for thinking? I have no talent.
          Never learned it. No use for it, really.
          I might just go ahead and shoot myself.
          Take the quick way out. Why not.
          What's to stop me? Life – an endless list
          Of uncertainties.

(shoots himself)

———

Scene 2

*(**enter** Superintendent **Pratt**, police officer **Hoyle**)*

PRATT   I don't know what to make of it.
          What do *you* make of it?

HOYLE   This is our third visit to the scene of the crime, Super.
          Why do we keep coming back?
          There's nothing more to be learned here.
          The man shot himself.
          Is it up to us to ask why?

PRATT   That's like saying: The law is a gimmick.
          No, the law is all we have, Hoyle.
          Without the law we are no longer in the
          Supply chain of your ordinary organic being.
          Any road up, it's not due to me.
          Orders come from higher up.
          Of course we have a modicum of wriggle room.
          It's up to us to say the corpse should stay
          Or the corpse should be taken away,
          Buried, autopsied, embalmed, salted, what do I care.

4

	I never shrug off the final decision.
	It makes me feel important and
	That is what life is about.
	That's evidently what this poor bugger was missing.
	Look at him. Look at that meaningless grin,
	As if he were saying: It was my birthday today
	And nobody noticed. Nooobody noticed.
	Aw heck, it brings tears to your eyes, don't it.
HOYLE	Have you had lunch yet?
PRATT	Lunch? No. I mean yes. No, I'm not hungry.
HOYLE	Say what you mean, Super. I'm easy.
PRATT	That's not the point is it! Whether you're easy!
	Your day will come, don't you know that?
	Nobody gets away with it forever.
HOYLE	*He* did. Look at him. Not a worry in the world.
	He's a memory now, for anyone.
	Anyone who likes can remember him and say:
	I'm glad I have at least that memory.
	Of him. Access to the dead, like.
PRATT	I wonder might you be running over at the mouth.
HOYLE	No, honestly, Super. It just now occurred to me.
	It could be that dead people are around for a reason.
	In sum, they amount to the magic blanket called
	History. What is history? Ruins. Believe it.
	You say that law is all we have?
	No, we also have history. We have our memory.
	That corpse there has inspired me
	To think creatively about the human condition.
PRATT	Well, like I said: We have wriggle room.
	However, in all good conscience,
	We do get that pay-check.

5

So let's try to earn it.
Here, grab hold. Let's pull that thing off the stage.
People don't like to be reminded of death.
Although, here's the thing,
As soon as you look at that, at that corpse …
Well, it's not dead, is it. A corpse isn't dead.
A person is dead, suddenly like,
But then, just as suddenly, there's that corpse,
And there's no such thing as a dead corpse.
After all, have you ever seen a living corpse?
Well, that would be a manner of speech, then.
The way you say to someone: You look like a
Corpse warmed up today, what's wrong with you?

HOYLE   There you go, Super. Inspiration. You too.
But you're right. Grab a hold. Let's transport
This perfectly respectable corpse off the stage,
Just in case someone ever does phone up and ask:
By the way, has anyone seen What's his name?

*(**Pratt** and **Hoyle** exit with the corpse in tow)*

Scene 3

*(the two **Gentlemen** enter)*

GENT.2   Or look at it this way.
From what you were saying earlier.
Abigail, you recall. She phoned? Yes?
Try to look at me when I'm talking to you, old chap.
Or has the rot set in? Yes, Abigail.
Try to guess what she wanted.
Why did she want me to join her? Go ahead.
This will give you an idea of the ideal marriage.

GENT.1   She needed you to pare her corns.

6

GENT.2	No. Way off the mark. Try again.
GENT.1	Oh dear! Conjugal duties, etcetera, was it?
GENT.2	Noo, nooo! Way off the mark. I'll tell you.
	It had occurred to her she needed a present
	For her mother on her birthday.
	Every year the two of us get together over that.
	So we discussed it at length –
	And decided to knit her a few doilies.
GENT.1	Get off it! You're pulling my leg!
GENT.2	Not knit, sorry, crochet.
	Side by side we sat for the rest of the afternoon,
	Pleasant conversation, crocheting away,
	And at nine we had four place mats.
GENT.1	I thought you said doilies.
GENT.2	We changed our mind. Besides, it's the same.
	Doilies, placemats. What does it matter?
	The quality time, that's what matters.
	You see, that's the trouble with you.
	You worry about the difference between
	Placemats and doilies, so you miss the point.
GENT.1	By the way, did you read it in the Chronicle?
	That I'd shot myself?
GENT.2	Yes, three days ago. What was that about?
	Were you really that fed up?
GENT.1	To be honest, it came over me – after our talk.
	Could think of no reason to carry on.
GENT.2	So what now? Clean slate?
GENT.1	The existence of a corpse is nothing to
	Write home about. It makes a fellow sullen.
GENT.2	Sullen, eh. Who would have thought!
	Well, take another crack at it.

Tell you what. Take up crocheting,
Then join Abigail and me for a pleasant afternoon.
She asks about you.
Wondered why you'd shot yourself.
I couldn't explain it.

GENT 1:   In the end it was worth it.
I'll not go on about it. Just to say:
Being dead is meaningless, that's all.
But it's also an affront to the living.
Makes them wonder why the sun shines.
I'll not do it again. I'll not make a habit of it.
You may count on me, in future.

GENT.2   So glad to hear it! Be cheerful!
Even in the face of death, be cheerful.
You've nothing to blame yourself for.
Besides, guilt is an eye-opener.

GENT.1   Did you know that a police Superintendent
And his sidekick dragged the corpse off the stage?
Oh yes. I had lain there for three days,
Not smelling any sweeter on the third day,
I can tell you, and they performed that service.
The audience had begun to fidget.

GENT.2   After three days, I should think so!

GENT.1   That insignificant act of kindness –
That was what brought me back to life.

GENT.2   I see! I see now! Splendid!
That had completely passed me by.
I must say – well – excellent!
I must tell Abigail.

GENT.1   Yes. Do tell Abigail. I have noticed
That women understand that sort of thing.

GENT.2   You mean like corpses coming back to life?

GENT.1   No, no. I mean little acts of kindness.
          The feminine heart thrives on them.
          I believe you may take it for granted
          That when you tell her what I said
          She will put down her crocheting,
          She will rise out of her chair, come over to you
          And kiss you gently upon the forehead.

GENT.2   How sweet! Yes, I will tell her.

                    (his telephone rings)

          Wait, that will be her on the phone again.
          'Yes dear. You what! That's astonishing!
          All by yourself? Then you did what?
          I don't believe it! What a marvel you are!
          Oh yes, of course, I'll be with you in the
          Shake of a lamb's tail.'
          There you go, old chap.
          She's done it again. Must go.
          What is life, eh? A necklace –
          And every pearl is a miracle.
          Stay well. No more trips to the morgue,
          Do you hear me?

                    (Gent. 2 *leaves)*

GENT.1   Well, that's more like it.
          Back among the living,
          Making my little contribution,
          Wishing everyone well –
          What's not to like about that?
          I believe this fellow will actually
          Dance off he stage.

                (Gent. 1 *dances off the stage)*

                    _____

Act 1

Scene 1

(On stage, around the perimeter, almost out of sight, are all the players who will eventually choose roles for themselves.)

TREVOR   It's possible to be so god-damned comfortable,
So self-satisfied – put it that way – that it seems like
Too much effort even to want to be human.
If it doesn't fall into our lap
We've no use for it.
You, sir, from the audience,
Are you too satisfied to want to be human?

A MEMBER of the AUDIENCE

       (mumbles something)

TREVOR   Sorry? No, don't be embarrassed.
Come up here. Tell everybody.
Are you too …

MEMBER   *(joins Trevor on the stage)*
That's okay, I heard you. Relax a bit.

TREVOR   Sorry?

MEMBER   I said: Relax a bit. I heard you.
Too self-satisfied to want to be human?
It's a sort of formula you've come up with, is it?
Very nice. Now you want me to respond?

TREVOR   If it's not too much trouble?

MEMBER   Alright. I will. Too much trouble?
Yes, I'm too busy, really.
That's it in a nutshell.
Besides, why should anyone want to be human?
It's a stupid question. We're born human.

10

There, that's my answer.
Can I sit down again?

TREVOR   Yes of course. Thank you. Well done. Oh dear!

(**Member of Audience** *returns to his seat*)

This means we have to redefine our purpose.
(*thinks*) Make-belief, that's the thing.
We will make him believe what we want him to believe.
Why will we do that? (*thinks*) I really don't know.
We will enjoy doing it? – There!
Now then, let me see, how about:
A pair of star-cross'd lovers take their life
And with their death bury…

A HELPER   (*runs up to him, whispers*)

TREVOR   What?

HELPER   (shouts) It's been done!

TREVOR   Oh, right. Sorry. How about:
In Africa a distraught mother
Kills her child who accidentally
spilled that week's supply of water …

HELPER   (*runs up to him, whispers*)

TREVOR   Is it! Oh for Pete's sake!
Somewhere in the middle then.
Five starlings represent the issues of the day
And sing solutions to intractable problems.
Well? What say you to that, Mr. Know-it-all?
Nothing? Very well, nothing!
Two-thousand years of modernity,
Masses of drama, drama, drama
And nothing substantial for the stage?
Are we to believe that? Make-belief?
It looks like I will have to step into the breech.

11

Players! On the stage, please.

(all the players come into view)

Up to you to improvise 'the life'.
We want the life that holds when the conditions
For modern life become too frail and brittle.
Show us what happens when the eternal life
Knocks on the door, the window, the brick wall
And none come forth from within and shout:
Quick! Enter!
Show us how we, in our too busy lives,
Are rendered helpless by the very help
That draws us, here, within our secret parts –
That urges us, with diverse pain and sickness,
With jealousy, with madness, insane rage,
To take advantage of our heritage,
To learn that every man contains good spirit,
That every woman's wisdom rests within
Her individual knowledge of nobility
And nothing dares disturb the female will,
The male justice, but there's grief to pay.

Right! So much for that.
Now we have some decisions to make.
I suggest we begin with a kind of chorus,
A handful of players who maker suggestions and
comments – helpful hindrances, etcetera.
Lorrain, Annie, and maybe you, Rita,
If you don't mind, the female part of the chorus.
Ted, Carl and Frank, will you take the male contingent?
Good. Fine. That, at least, is settled.
You play yourselves. You continue to invent yourselves.
Think of ourselves as the soil in which we root.
The magic six. The lower and the
upper limit, so to speak.

12

	Now let's see what happens.

Now let's see what happens.
All the other roles will have to
Rise out of the occasion of the initial chorus.
That's how I see it at the moment.
Off you go.
(*Trevor steps back*)

LORRAINE   Lorraine has an idea.
Why don't we take up the struggle
Between the caring few and the crowd of the lost
And gradually shape it into …

TED   No! Ted says no. You and your ideas!
Trevor just dealt with that.
The bit about the starlings.
Did you not understand that?

LORRAINE   No I didn't, smartass.
Maybe you'd like to explain?

TED   It shouldn't be necessary.
It's so obvious!
You don't explain a symbol.

TRISH   (*comes on*) Alright, you two.
Always at each other's throats.
I agree that we should
Leave the starlings on their perch.
Now and then a murmuration,
But you can get too much of a good thing.
I see myself as a courtesan;
No, better, as the scheming wife of a meek husband.
I scheme because it gives me pleasure
And I've not yet learned the consequences.
Here, Alphonse!
(*to the player who happily agrees to play Alphonse*)
You have too much free time on your hands.
That's what's wrong with you.

Of course you don't agree with me. Why should you!

TREVOR   *(comes on)* You name, please?

TRISH   My name? Trish. Short for Patricia.

ALPHONSE   Yes dear, you are quite right. But there's nothing to do.
             Alphonse can't very well pretend to be busy just to
             please you. My survival instincts tell me: Relax! There's
             money in the bank. My health is good. Circumstances
             flatter my ego. In other words: Drift through the day.
             I make some minimal effort not to fall asleep in my
             chair here – Could we have an easy-chair, please! Quick!

HELPER   *(comes on, brings a chair, goes off)*

ALPHONSE   Thank you. *(sits)* Now if I might insist upon a little
             gratitude for my minimal effort not to fall asleep in my
             chair during the day?

TRISH   Oh dear! I believe it's high time for me to scour the
             horizon for a little extra erotic stimulus. All work and
             no play makes Trish a dissatisfied minx.

ALPHONSE   Oh by all means, Trish. Be my guest. Did you say work?
             I snicker. Just perceptibly I snicker. What you call work
             I call self-indulgence. What you call self-indulgence
             I call perverse delight taken in the misfortunes of
             the voting public.

TREVOR   *(comes on)*
             Enough marital bickering please.
             It becomes tiresome.
             (leaves)

UNCLE WERNER *(comes on)*
             Here we go. Uncle Werner to the rescue.
             I see myself as Uncle Werner and actually I am
             A little excited to find out where that will lead.
             My dear Trish, you have mentioned the need for

14

Erotic stimulus. I will be more than pleased
To put you in touch with an interesting friend of mine,
A sportsman, a tennis player, retired.
Goes by the name of Vivian Clough,
Perhaps you've heard of him.
Good company at the worst of times
And won't get in the way when things go well.
Give me the nod and I'll set up a meeting.

TRISH Oh that's priceless, Uncle.
A retired sportsman.
What say you to that, Alphonse?

ALPHONSE Oh go for it. Go for it, Trish.
It will take the pressure off me.

ANNIE Typical unresponsive husband –
Won't take the bait.
Won't rise to the occasion.
Don't you realize what's going on here?
You're supposed to get mad!
Why don't you fight?

TED Why don't you leave him alone?
He *is* fighting, aren't you Alphonse?
You're fighting a rearguard action.
We men have our own way of coping.

ALPHONSE Now now. Don't assume you know me.
I'm not one of your team-players, you know,
Teaming up with other males against the female.

TRISH Well, thank you for that, husband.

LORRAINE Oh come on, you're letting him get away with that?
You are letting the side down badly, girl.

TRISH I'll show you what side I'm on as soon as I meet
Uncle Werner's tennis player, retired.

15

	I dare say, Uncle, he still has a
	Fast first serve, ho ho?
	How about his back-hand volley?
UNCLE	A nobleman, a noble man, of the old vintage.
	You'll see. His conversation is as good as it gets.
	He will spear you a witticism and
	Serve it cold at the exact precise moment.
GALINA	*(comes on)*
	I do know who you mean, Uncle.
	He used to bring me flowers after every performance.
	Had a passion for the ballet.
	Never asked for favours.
TREVOR	*(comes on)* Your name please, dear?
GALINA	Galina, I believe. Yes, Galina. There was, at one time …
	No, never mind, that's beside the point.
	Just Galina. Has a lovely ring to it.
	(to Uncle Werner) What was his name again, Uncle?
UNCLE W.	Vivian Clough, dear.
GALINA	Yes, he was very attentive. Supportive even.
ANNIE	Oh oh! There you have him, Trish.
	An empty vessel.
	An admirer of appearances.
	An aestheticist, no less. No more, either, of course.
	An obscenity with the pants down.
CARL	There she goes again.
	Why don't you listen to your conscience for once!
	You've the birds and the bees on the brain.
GALINA	He always behaved honourably, that's the point.
	Besides, ballerinas commonly choose to abide by
	A certain code of conduct. It's just not practical
	To get bogged down in affairs. One travels, you know.

ALPHONSE   Good for you, Galina. By the way,
I hope you are keeping up your exercises.
A break from performing can lead to cramps.

UNCLE   He's right, Galina.
But tell me this: Would you be happy enough
To meet Vivian again, if I were to invite him?

GALINA   Oh more than happy, Uncle!
It was always a treat for me to be with him.
What a good idea! Trish, Alphonse –
Do let's invite him some evening.
Uncle Werner will ask him,
And you'll let him know that I will be here,
Won't you, Uncle.

TREVOR   (comes on) Very good, people.
Let's call that Scene One, why don't we.
A short rest, then scene two, alright?
By the way, there's something I haven't told you.
Jeremy set up hidden cameras before we started,
So your performances will be on record.

ALL PLAYERS
    Oh fine! Great! Excellent! Brilliant! (etc.)

———

Scene 2

(All the players provide a supportive background.)

TREVOR   So what we need at the beginning of Scene Two
Is an player who will do Vivian Clough.

A PLAYER   *(the player who will do V. C. comes forward)*
How about me. You mean the tennis player?

TREVOR   Well, if you want to put it that way.
I suppose he doesn't really exist

17

	Until we have someone to play that role. But you've heard of him, have you?
PLAYER	Goodness me, who hasn't! World number one for ten years, Wimbledon champion three times. But he drinks now. To Excess. Pity.
LORRAINE	(*from the background*) What? Water?
PLAYER	No, alcohol, silly!
UNCLE	(*steps forward to join Trevor*)

Excuse me for butting in here but
I had actually conceived him as
A noble man. Forgive me, it's an uncommon
Description of anyone nowadays
But his attitude to life is most peculiar.
You might play him as someone who
Automatically thinks of someone else
Before thinking of himself.
I mean under pressure.

(*he steps back again*)

PLAYER	That's odd. He would have to stop stupefying himself With numberless cocktails and ...
TREVOR	Oh no, can't have that. That's up to you then – If you take the role. Also it might not be wise to imagine That some actual Vivian Clough exists. We make him up, is that understood? I don't believe in imitative acting. That's just pretending, really, isn't it.
PLAYER	I certainly hadn't heard of Vivian Clough Until Uncle Werner mentioned the name, So have no fear.

His nobility will shine clear.

TREVOR   Not exactly what I meant.
Anyway, will you play him then?

PLAYER   I will conjure him in masterful fashion.

TREVOR   Excellent. What I have in mind now
Is that you and Uncle Werner will do this next scene.
Will you be able to handle that?
At such short notice?

PLAYER   Now that is what I call a rush-job.
Uncle Werner has not dealt fairly
And squarely with me in the past.
He nurses the prejudice that actors are less than human.
From case to case that may fit
But as a generality it won't wash.
However, I'll do my best.

TREVOR   Thank you. Uncle Werner,
Will you join us now please?

VIVIAN   Oh the dreaded thought of having to make allowances
For someone who cackles like a chicken and
Croaks like a frog! However, what's the life of an actor.
The sheer crack of doom overwhelms at times.

TREVOR   *(Uncle Werner steps for ward again to join Trevor and
Vivian Clough)*

Here we are then. Vivian Clough, Uncle Werner.
Uncle Werner, Vivian Clough.
Shall we get to know one another?
You both know me as the director
Who wishes to put on a serious play called:
The Modern Drama. An indicative title, to be sure.
Am I right in assuming you two have never met?

UNCLE W. Not met, but I've watched you play, there.

19

	Most entertaining. I refer especially to the
	Four and a half hour contest against …
VIVIAN	Oh, don't mention that one! I played poorly.
	If I recall correctly, my shoulder gave me trouble
	And someone in the stands kept heckling,
	Calling me obscene names, and the like.
	Calculated to make a fellow throw in the towel.
UNCLE W.	It wasn't me, although …
TREVOR	Well, that's by the by.
	For all I care you may be sworn enemies.
	The play is the thing that wants to come into being.
	You will improvise to your hearts' content.
	So far both Trish and Alphonse have done a sterling job.
	I intend that our males and females
	Will continue to provide the chorus lines, ha!
	Galina is a late arrival. She maintains that
	You, Vivian, used to attend her performances and
	Bring her gifts, is that correct?
VIVIAN	Galina! A truly wonderful dancer!
	It will be a thrill to meet her again.
	We were the closest of friends while we met.
	Afterwards, each time, we broke off entirely.
	That worked for us. An ideal liaison.
	She may not recognize me now.
TREVOR	Well, we shall see. Your …
VIVIAN	I have changed since our last outing.
	She may, in fact, look at me and say: Who are you?
	And that would break my heart.
	I mean it would wound my vanity.
	Same thing, eh?
TREVOR	Don't worry, it will all …

VIVIAN	Then again, she may have changed too – Does she still do her exercises?
TREVOR	We must move on!
LORRAINE	(from the perimeter) Stay flexible, Trevor!
UNCLE W.	Yes, Vivian, we must move on. The world does not rotate around your Wonderful affair with Galina.
VIVIAN	No, of course not. Thank you for reminding me. I will have to work hard now To keep that beloved name in perspective.
TREVOR	You will succeed, I know you will. The time has come for cobbling together our next scene. Don't forget, this is only the beginning. Modernity is a precious concept. It has a nasty way of interfering with our Contemporary perception of time. I dare say our play will draw more and more Attention to that as we make headway.

Scene 3

*(**Trevor, Trish, Alphonse, Galina, Vivian Clough**
 plus some of the **Chorus** in the foreground, later **Miriam**.
 The rest in the background)*

TREVOR	So, here we all are, all together Inside the same sleeping bag, as it were. Do we have our willing males and females? Yes? Good. You will participate as the play dictates. We go for depth now. And keep in mind, please, The secret mysteries of the depth –

Keep them hidden on the surface, as usual.
We cater to a mixed audience.
Trish, will you start us off, please?

TRISH   Gladly. All the more gladly because today –
Today I am walking around with a head like
A grizzly bear. It happens. Please be careful.
Meanwhile I will try to overcome with gladness.
I slept poorly last night. In my mind I was
Scheming. Yes, scheming. Alphonse and I –
This may come as a bit of a shock –
Are hoping to adopt a child.
We have not mentioned that to anyone.
However we agreed to mention it today.
Alphonse, please stand beside me here
So that I can feel your support.
(*Alphonse obediently moves to Trish's side*)
We gladly admit we are both scared.
What about? A good question.
Are we up to having children, I suppose
That's the main worry. Will we be able to
Behave like mature adults and not like
Self-conscious adolescents or like
Headstrong know-it-alls.
At the orphanage we were told we had to
Fill out umpteen forms and attend umpteen
Meetings with …

A PLAYER   Oh I can help you there. I can make things
Easy for you. I will hand over my little
Tim to you just like that, no questions asked.

ALPHONSE   I beg your pardon?

PLAYER   I mean it. I didn't want him in the first place.
I was raped. But I didn't want an abortion.
So I thought I'd see how it goes.

	He's two years old and a bit
	And he's hardly been mistreated much at all.
	I can let you have him for the sum of …
	Oh, let me see – I'll pay you a hundred pounds.
	I'll throw in the play pen and the Lego set; almost new.

TRISH   You're joking!

PLAYER   I'm not, Trish. I can't afford him any longer.
There's no more help from the government.
I work ten hours a day at the supermarket.
He spends all that time at a so-called playschool
And who knows what all goes on there.
You take him. Bring him up. I'll visit once a year,
From Alaska, his favourite aunt. Bring him presents.
You know, those smooth carvings of sea lions,
He'll love those.

TREVOR   And who are you, dear? We haven't met you yet.

PLAYER   Oh right. Sorry. Let me see. I feel like a Miriam.
Plenty of 'previous' there, I realize that.
Maybe I can capitalize on it.
Miriam. Is that alright?

TREVOR   (*motions to her to continue*)

ALPHONSE   Seems like a win-win situation to me, Trish.
Miriam gets her life back, the child …

MIRIAM   Tim!

ALPHONSE   Tim – thank you – gets a proper home and …

MIRIAM   I was not, by the way, suggesting there was anything
Improper, as such, about his present home.

ALPHONSE   Sorry, Miriam. Bad choice of words. He will have
More of a family now – will that do? – and
Trish and I have not, so far, been impressed by

	Those children at the orphanage.
TED	Mind you, you haven't met little Tim.
CARL	And he'll not be properly your own, will he. Especially if Miriam comes to visit. She'd still be his real mother.
TRISH	You are talking about something there That makes no real sense to me. What about you, Alphonse?
ALPHONSE	All I can say is We would do our best to be his real parents. And if Miriam wants to help a little, good! I would say, with all due respect to M2, you are introducing the element of nonsense.
TREVOR	If I can come in here, you will have to get Legal transfer papers drawn up. Shall I contact a solicitor for you?
ALPHONSE	What do you say, Trish? I'm for it.
TRISH	Yes, by all means, let's do it. How fortunate that we decided to mention this today! Why don't you visit us along with Tim a few times, Miriam, so that he'll get used to us, and then our home will become his.
MIRIAM	Brilliant idea! Starting tomorrow, if you're agreeable. Tomorrow's Sunday.
TREVOR	By the way, I wouldn't be greatly in favour of Bringing a two-year-old child onto this stage; If you can keep that in mind, please, as the play goes on. When he's into his adolescence, then, maybe.
TRISH	Fair enough, Trevor. It shouldn't become necessary.
TREVOR	Well, it's up to us, isn't it?

TRISH   What? Oh alright, fair enough.

TREVOR   Well isn't it? Look, I have to make sure that
              No one here is labouring under a misapprehension
              Of the dramatic process as realist or reductive.
              If little Tom, or Tim, should ever decide –
              I mean once the hormones start to pump –
              To make his presence felt on the stage –
              In life, I mean – that would be up to him
              And it would be wrong of us to get in his way.

ALPHONSE   Yes, Trevor. Alright already. Understood.

TREVOR   No, I'm sorry, but you still make it sound as if
              My own personal weal and woe depended on
              How we manage our verbal transactions.
              It just plain ain't so! I don't like to badger you
              But we have to get down to the nitty-gritty nowadays.
              The choice is ours, elemental or realistic.
              Do we make our ...

VIVIAN CLOUGH (*comes forward*)
              Trevor, sorry, but I have to come in here.
              You are, at present, going against your own principles.
              You are shouting in the cellar what you ought to be
              Whispering in the conservatory. On a sunny day.
              I know what I'm talking about.
              I have suffered unaccountably from this
              Miserable duality most of my life, and I've learned:
              Nobody can take this on as an individual.
              That's what you are trying to do right now.

TREVOR   Well, good to see you here, Vivian.
              It looks like I'll have to take myself to task.
              It's a case of 'go with the flow', I guess.
              But you all know what I'm worried about, don't you.
              It's the blather.

25

And the structure imposed from outside.
We are not involved here in skeleton-decoration.

VIVIAN   So let's do it and not talk it.
For a start, where is Galina?
I was told she'd be here today.
Trevor, you and Uncle Werner promised.

GALINA   (*comes forward*)
Right on cue, Vivian.
It's a pleasure to see you again.
We should have kept in touch, don't you think?
Why didn't we, I wonder.

VIVIAN   My dear. What a treat this is!
There was always too much at stake.
Now that my good wife has passed on
We can recommence our relationship on a new footing.

GALINA   Yes of course. How insensitive of me.
I had forgotten how she was ill for years.
You were always so careful not to do anything
That would disturb her ease.
And now she's gone. You are a free man.

VIVIAN   Oh now, I was a free man then too,
However not at liberty to take up with another woman.

GALINA   Of course. Pardon me. Words are important.
You are at liberty to become my closest possible friend,
Am I right?

TED   This is about to turn into a soap opera

CARL   Except the language is a bit complicated.

VIVIAN   As much as I would like to speak in favour of
Soap operas, I find myself constrained to concentrate
On my own list of preferences here.
I see several unfamiliar faces.

Trevor. Do your duty, please.

TREVOR   Yes, or course. Pardon me. As the director of the drama
          I should have introduced them to you right away.
          Trish and Alphonse are with us for a short stay
          From Peru, where they have made themselves
          responsible for a cocoa plantation. They have just
          a few minutes ago decided to adopt Miriam's child.
          This is Miriam. Allow me once again to introduce
          Vivian Clough to you all.
          He comes highly recommended.

ANNIE   Which means what?

GALINA   Have you taken lodgings in town, Vivian?
          We must get together. Of course you can join me
          At my hotel, but I cannot recommend the food,
          So before you leave we must decide on a place.

FRANK   She's a fast worker. And thorough. Hat's off.

VIVIAN   Now! Where is your Uncle Werner?
          He promised to be here. I want to ask him about his
          Bee-keeping skills. Did you know that he has
          Written a very clever book about bees,
          Rivalled only by Maeterlink's 'Life of the Bees'.

RITA   Is this really a fact or are you making this up?

GALINA   We learn one another's secrets so late, or not at all.

TREVOR   How very true. No one until now has ever been told
          That I killed my sister when I was sixteen.
          Yes, no wonder you look shocked.
          I can recall every minute detail of it
          And I feel not the least regret. How strange that is!

GALINA   Would it be wise of you to tell us more?

TREVOR   Periodically throughout my life I have been visited

By the most lifelike dreams, not at night but in the
Light of day. At such times I bear no resemblance to my
Usual self – from my own point of view, of course.
An irresistible attraction to the art of drama
Springs from such repeated experiences.
It is almost as if I were hoping to be able to harness
The energy that drives such irresponsible acts
To some creative process that would help people
Cling less adamantly to the things of the world.

VIVIAN   My dear sir, is it your intention here to confess?

TREVOR   See if you can imagine how <u>you</u> might have felt
If during a performance of the Chopin piano concerto
A young man in the row in front of you had suddenly
Leapt up on his chair and shouTED
No one can understand the truth of this music!

TRISH   You did this, Trevor?

TREVOR   No, but someone who impersonated me, Trish.
The poor man was bustled out or the auditorium
And I came to my senses in the ambulance that
Transported me to a hospice for the deranged.
'What am I doing here?' I wanted to know.
'How did I get here?' When the awful scene was
Described to me I had no memory of it.
Usually enough evidence remained to speak for itself,
Otherwise I might have accused the world of madness.

ANNIE   Such great sadness!
That one should have to live with it!

TREVOR   Since I have devoted myself to the discipline of the
Dramatic art, I have remained unmolested.

TED   'Thank God for that' is all I can say.

TREVOR   And there we have to leave it for today.

You will be glad to hear that our dear Uncle Werner
Is waiting for the seven of us at the pub across the street.

LORRAINE Right, we will tidy up as usual, Trevor.
You can count on the six of us to make ourselves
Useful in your absence.

TREVOR My faith in you all knows no bounds.
You are the true Chorus.
The voice of the hidden god.
If only people realized how …

VIVIAN Oh come on, Trevor.
(takes him by the hand and leads him off)

TREVOR I only want to let them know how much they are
Appreciated, surely that's …

(his voice fades out as Vivian leads him away.)

———————

Scene 4

[the **Chorus**, (the *three* **males** *and the three* **females**]

LORRAINE They've sloped off to the pub and we stay behind.
This is how it should be. What possible use are we
When it comes to intelligent conversation, or when
Sympathy and compassion are the order of the day?

TED Yes, quite right. It's not as if we needed
Their company to enjoy ourselves.
We would only talk at cross purposes
And draw their displeasure down on our heads.

ANNIE There's a lot to be said for never having developed
Because obviously when something hurts us
We know how to help ourselves by finding the cause
And giving it the full treatment of our blame.

TED Oh you can say that again. I hate those complications

29

When those who have no conscience pretend
That they have one, so they tie themselves up in knots
With the result of a foul mood and gastric ulcers.

RITA   I owned a pet canary for many years and it sang
When sunshine was reflected on its cage
And as soon as a cloud passed over the sun
It stopped singing and perched there quietly.

FRANK   And that's what you're like, is that what you're saying?

RITA   Yes, that's what I'm like. That's what I'm saying.
It's only when I'm around Them that I have to
Pick on them, quarrel with them, make barbed comments,
Demonstrate my inconvenience over nothing as if
My importance were a thing that I could identify.

TED   That's exactly what I'm like. It's like an ache,
A painful pressure here in my chest when I
Hear them talk and its over my head, so I have to
Let them know that, somehow, I don't know why …

LORRAINE   Except that it makes you feel good, right?
It brings the energy up from below and you
Spit it out neat, which is sort of thrilling.

CARL   Yeah, it's adrenalin, you have to get rid of it.
They absorb it, although most of the time they
Don't let on, because of what they call manners.

ANNIE   Even right now I can feel the boredom coming on
Because there's nobody to criticize, especially
Secretly, before you make a sour face in response
To some suggestion one of them has made.

FRANK   It's true, isn't it. I've heard them say they can
Rejuvenate themselves by thinking – well, I have to
Take their word for it, because thinking only makes me
Cranky, and nervous; finally downright miserable.

30

RITA	So naturally you don't do it. You make sure you Stay away from it, right? They can do it for us. Some of them are good at it, some not so good. Here, we haven't swept the floor yet. Let's get on with it before they come back and Make us feel guilty,
TED	Which is a bad trip altogether, right?
LORRAINE	Yeah. A bad trip. Look, Trevor has left his orange behind.
CARL	Eat it. He won't miss it.
ANNIE	Nah, he won't miss it.
FRANK	Mind you he doesn't miss much.
RITA	Yeah, he doesn't miss much. (*yawns*)

Scene 5
*(in the pub, **Trevor, Trish, Alphonse,***
Miriam, Galina, Vivian** and **Uncle Werner;
now and again a waiter replenishes the wine glasses.)

UNCLE W.	What kept you all? I thought you were never coming.
TREVOR	Oh that play! It went on and on. It's as if we had grown into it now. I make no more excuses, I go until it feels right to stop. I have to say that my own personal convictions play a role all the time, albeit a subsidiary manner. And at the same time I know that I'm not on my own. I have to keep that in mind, that I'm not on my own. When I lose track, things go wrong – and go bad. Or rather – let me put it this way – when something goes wrong, or I get stuck, then I can be sure that I've lost track of – well, the companion. I call the one who is part of the equation, along with me, the companion.

31

GALINA	It's so fascinating! The very fact that I'm a dancer makes me light on my feet. You'd think it would have to be the other way around. And Vivian, you have your feet on the ground, that's for sure. When and where did we meet, by the way? Can you recall? It was after one of my performances, I'm sure of that. But where? Can you remember?
VIVIAN	Of course I can. I had just left military service, at the age of twenty-eight. I had taken a bullet in the left lung and that was slow to heal so I took up my hobby again, which was the collection and study – well, mostly the study – of the Precambrian fossil record. I published a few papers, attended conferences, travelled the world like a seed on wings and came upon you at Lady Potter's Ballet Centre in Australia. I confess I was hooked. You were still a girl, really, and obviously immensely talented. It was my first and lasting experience of feminine beauty. I married then, my Diana, and we raised four children. Then I came across you again at the height of your career, where was it, in Los Angeles, I believe, yes, Falstaff, where you showed off your contralto as Mistress Quickly – otherwise not a good choice for you, I thought. Shortly after that my wife became ill and I was unwilling to travel so much. When I saw you in Sleeping Beauty then, in New York, I looked you up. I presented my flowers, like a good boy, and you were kind enough to grant me an audience. That was the time. In New York. Five years ago. And that's my story.
GALINA	Thank you. I recall that you told me of your wife's unfortunate illness.
MIRIAM	Which was what, Vivian, if you don't mind my asking?
VIVIAN	She had lost the will to live, can you imagine that? A specialist in nerve ailments explained it to me in this

way. A series of the most puzzling weaknesses afflicted her, always to the point of near-total disability. She malingered, Miriam. And do you know what? I could not help but see this as the direct opposite of my own irrepressible vitality. After a time I even wondered did we react against each other. She fled from my vitality and I from her malaise.

UNCLE W.   That's astonishing, Vivian. And nothing could be done to reverse this process?

TREVOR   Quite right, Uncle. Is that not the first thought that occurs to us! Why does knowledge in such cases not result in ameliorative action. But Vivian will tell you, I'm sure, even as I understand it, that neither modern medicine nor modern philosophy, biology, psychology – you name it – has come up with, indeed cannot come up with, any solutions to such an elementary existential problem.

ALPHONSE   I think of it like this: It's impossible to fix the roof from inside the house.

VIVIAN   Ah, very clever! One has to hire a 'roofer', is that not what they're called? Which takes us back to the companion you mentioned at the start, Trevor. Not a 'modern' helper, is he.

TREVOR   One gets the impression he would like to be, however our unwillingness is all too fashionable.

TRISH   If a woman looks for him in her husband, is she misguided?

TREVOR   Only if she looks for him <u>as</u> her husband.

TRISH   Good point. How elegantly we are solving the modern predicament!

MIRIAM   I have to confess that while I may be learning something, I can contribute nothing in relation to this topic.

TRISH	Surely wisdom is required to know even that much.
MIRIAM	Thank you for that, Patricia. I have forgiven the man who raped me, don't you know. I learned that I was not alone in my predicament. I had companions. We conversed. The collective conclusion was: They can kill our body but not our soul, so why get frantic about it.
TREVOR	Surely that's a mature attitude.
MIRIAM	It also allowed me to become smarter in my relations with the male gender. A definite enlightenment came over me and over many of my sisters in grief. We understood that the male sexuality can present as much of a catastrophe as the female sexuality. The verdict, in the end, was: We can help one another out.
TREVOR	You mean males and females can help each other?
MIRIAM	Men and women, I dare say. We have to mature a little first.
GALINA	A decided improvement on the war of sexes, would you say?
MIRIAM	Indeed. And not to be mistaken for feminism, which I have come to understand, by the way, as the reluctance to learn how to be feminine.
TRISH	So do you suppose that males and females could learn how to become masculine and feminine?
ALPHONSE	They would have to be shown. Surely it's the sort of thing we can only learn by example. Virtue, in the absence of good examples, deteriorates and is turned into a legal and political right.
TREVOR	And how, after all, would you define virtue nowadays, Alphonse, when we suppose we can be good?

ALPHONSE	Let me think. – As the exercise of humanity and the practice of human being?
VIVIAN	Bravo, Alphonse!
TREVOR	Well, on that note ... I would call this 'improvisation at its best'. The wine was good too, Uncle. Will you all be available again tomorrow? At the theatre?
MIRIAM	I hope so. It's my Tim's last week at the playschool.
TRISH	Yes indeed! Trevor! We have made arrangements. Tomorrow afternoon the relevant papers will be signed, sealed and delivered.
TREVOR	Splendid! See you all tomorrow then. I foresee a bright future for little Tom. Or Tim, rather.

> *(the players depart severally, as they demonstrate their mutual affection)*

Scene 6

*(**Ted. Carl** and **Frank**; **Lorraine, Annie** and **Rita** at the theatre)*

LORRAINE	It's not as if we <u>had</u> to do this, don't you know. All the same, I find that sometimes I act as much off stage as on. Or maybe all I do is pretend.
ANNIE	There's a difference?
LORRAINE	Oh come on! Give me a break! Think of how you behave when you want your boyfriend to do this or that. When you want him to stop doing this or that. And let's pretend you're at a stage of the relationship where you've found out what works with him and what doesn't. You try to get your way, right? You don't come the heavy with him and say: Either you become more reliable or I cut off you wa-

ter! No, you practice little tricks, to make him feel things that, in your opinion, will smarten him up. You play Bambi or banshee and all the keys in between. But that's not acting is it.

ANNIE Alright then, what's acting?

TED Go ahead, Lorraine. You asked for it.

LORRAINE Well, I think of it as acting as though I meant it. When I act on stage I drive a bargain with myself. I cut out all my thoughts and feelings and become creative – whether I have a script or not. So I don't pose.

CARL When I act I let myself drift into a role and then I turn on it and take possession of it.

RITA There must be some relation to acting when we're off the stage. When we act during the day. Like when I do the dishes or type out an article or give a talk. Put it this way: I demonstrate personal energy – both on and off the stage.

FRANK Were you acting just now?

RITA Yes I was – but not for an audience. I was trying to get a point across. I believe I did it actively.

FRANK It seems to me that in the end this will boil down to the difference between art and realty. In both cases, if you want to be effective, to bring something about, you have to act. In both cases you do well to be creative. But you draw on a different spirit within yourself. Call it the art-spirit and the reality-spirit.

LORRAINE I like that. The art-spirit. Let's put that to the test. Shall we put that to the test?

TED Why not? Starting now?

LORRAINE	The thing is, if you don't behave you get smacked. You, you don't behave. The depression will set in. Wait till you see.
ANNIE	I'm being myself. I don't think you should criticize me. I'm not hurting anyone.
TED	She's right, Lorraine. You're upset because you were stood up. I don't blame you.
CARL	I was stood up the other day. I felt gutted. It was the first time. Best to get used to that, I guess.
FRANK	It's hard to get used to the fact that when we hurt, that doesn't mean that somebody intended to hurt us. Half the time when I get angry at somebody I should really be angry with myself.
RITA	I hate myself when I realize I've reacted again. It's so stupid! Why not think first, I tell myself. Why not wait five seconds before I open my mouth.
LORRAINE	Right. Now what about the following. Annie, with a face like yours you could have been a bus conductor.
ANNIE	How dare you! Is that supposed to be a joke?
TREVOR	*(comes on stage, observes without being seen)*
RITA	Oh my, look at her! If you can't take it get off the bus.
TED	Typical females. Sooner or later you get in each other's hair. You need men to keep you in line.
FRANK	That's right. What are they like on their own. Like cats. And so superficial. There's no depth to a woman.
ANNIE	I'm going to let that pass because I don't believe you mean that.
TED	There, you see? Right away the tears flow. So predictable!

37

CARL	Don't look at me. I want no part of this. I figure if people want to fight you have to let them get on with it. Myself, I just smile to myself and think: There but for my superior character go I. All the same, I think you should apologize, Lorraine. That was uncalled-for. Somebody with a face like Annie's should be mollycoddled, you know, pampered, to help her forget what she looks like.
LORRAINE	I remember a time, Carl, when you still cared.
CARL	That was when I was still being respected for being a person in my own right, not just an extension of some … what … well, an extension.
LORRAINE	You certainly look like an extension. Mind you, you always have. There's no centre to you, Carl. You bend with the wind. Then you snap.
CARL	You really are an obnoxious bitch!
LORRAINE	That's better than being a nothing. A vacuum! A waste of space!
ANNIE	I'm with Carl here. You're a wicked female, Lorraine.
TED	Oh here we go again. Into each other's hair.
RITA	That's it. Stand by and smirk. I hate your type. (**Rita** shoves **Ted,** he shoves back)
TREVOR	Here! What in the name… What's got into you lot? What kind of behaviour is that! I thought you were friends! Stop it!
CARL	Trevor! How long have you been watching? Did you not know we were acting?
TREVOR	It never entered my mind.
LORRAINE	That's interesting. I wonder what that tells us.
TREVOR	What were you trying to prove?

RITA   Nothing, really. We were trying to arrive at a definition of art-acting in comparison to real-acting.

TREVOR   Whatever could you be talking about? So did you learn anything?

TED   It appears that from the outside there's no detectable difference.

ANNIE   That's right. Only inwardly you cooperate with a different spirit.

TREVOR   The art-spirit, I take it?

LORRAINE Yes! That's it!

TREVOR   Oh dear! I wonder is this worth knowing.

RITA   It is for us, Trevor. Wait till you see. We've made a discovery and we'll benefit from it.

TREVOR   Well, glad to hear it. Now if it's alright with you, can we put together our next scene? Can you even remember where we left off last time?

LORRAINE Of course we can, Trevor. Life goes on regardless. And the invisible link is the strongest.

TREVOR   Whatever that means. Maybe I should just step out of the picture and let you lot carry on as you fit.

ANNIE   We imagined that's what you were doing all along.

———

Act II

Scene 1

(*Galina*, *at night*)

GALINA   I walked up and down in my bedroom because I couldn't
sleep. My mind was furiously turning over with I know
not what thoughts when suddenly I heard a voice. It
spoke to me but I understood nothing. I experienced a
tremendous agitation of my soul. It has never happened
before. I'm a rational human being.

VOICE   You should now be able to hear me.

GALINA   There it was again. Oh no, this is terrible!
What's happening to me? Am I going out of my mind?

VOICE   Listen. Only listen. And hear me.
You have only a little time left,
Then your life will be over.
If you do as I say you have nothing to fear.
Will you do as I say?

GALINA   What choice do I have?
My body feels as if it were trapped in a vice.
Why don't you show yourself?
Because I would scream?

VOICE   Everyone, not only you, has to be cleansed
of all that is modern. Modernity has spoiled you.
You are able to accept and hold what I will tell you.
Have nothing more to do with bad entertainments,
with your addiction to mass media, with your
endless concerns for your convenient survival.
Your human spirit wishes to reside in you safely,
No longer anxious about being betrayed by
fixations on extinct ideas, on mere images which
allow your self to proliferate endlessly.

40

GALINA   My heart is in my mouth.
           I feel a change coming over me.
           Who are you?

VOICE   I am an extension into you of good spirit.
           Find a way to bring those you know to their senses.
           This will be your personal mission.
           A completely new spirit will live in you.
           Learn how to make your peace with it
           And know that what it means is work.

GALINA   Why me? My life's work is finished.
           I was a dancer. I entertained all my life.
           How can I suddenly become ... what ...

VOICE   Gradually you will grow into it.
           Don't be afraid. You will have help where it is needed.
           Now make your peace with your new life.
           (*the voice is still*)

GALINA   Let's face it, I knew something like this was on the cards.
           I've only been pretending – for over a year.
           One puts it down to the advancing years,
           When in fact yet again good spirit changes us –
           But so abruptly! Why does it have to be so sudden?
           Well, I'd best stop arguing and get on with it.
           The new Galina – a fledgling again.
           Several times during my career my understanding
           Was turned upside down and I had the choice of
           Viewing it as an end or as a new beginning.
           But at my age!
           Well, do I know best?
           Hardly.
           The spirit that moves the stars moves me too.
           I will seek me out a companion,
           To share the responsibility.
           Oh really? And who would that be?

41

Certainly no one I can point at.
Certainly no one I could ever point out to the
Audience from the dance floor.
Enough said.

VOICE   You will know from day to day how to behave.

GALINA   Ah, yes of course.
Why try to figure it out ahead of time.
I will have a conversation with Vivian.
That will allow me to test the ground I still stand on.

Scene 2

*(**Galina**, **Vivian** at Vivian's apartment)*

GALINA   Vivian, have you time for me, at this unearthly hour?

VIVIAN   Why of course. This is an unexpected pleasure!
Please come in. Are you in some trouble?
Has something happened? – You do look a bit pale.

GALINA   Well, yes and no, Vivian. For the moment
I need someone I can trust to talk to.

VIVIAN   Well, then I'm ready to listen.
You'll be glad to know that I will
Not try to drag anything out of you.
Mind you, I would feel much better with a drink.
I will get that. I do feel a bit nervous. What about you?

GALINA   No thank you.
                    (Vivian leaves)
You feel nervous?
Wait until I tell you what happened to me.
But no. That would be wrong.
I have to play this by ear.
How can I possibly involve someone else in this!
But I must. I can't face it alone.

42

VIVIAN	(*comes back*)
	Here we go now. I'm strangely fidgety.
	It's as if I were about to sit an exam.
	I wonder why that is.
GALINA	Please believe that I don't wish to frighten you, Vivian,
	But have you ever thought at length about why you –
	Well – why you exist on this earth?
VIVIAN	You don't mean rather than on Mars or Pluto?
GALINA	I refer to the wider purpose of our existence.
	Oh how awkward does that sound! No, I mean
	Are you perfectly at ease in yourself, Vivian?
	Would you be quite happy to depart tomorrow?
VIVIAN	Would I have a choice?
GALINA	Of course not. But would you be content to go?
VIVIAN	If you put it like that – no. No I wouldn't.
GALINA	And can you say why not?
VIVIAN	A very difficult question.
	It brings to the surface a whole lot of things;
	a lot of unfinished business, I dare say.
	I believe I get the drift of what you are up to here, Galina.
	No I would not be content to go
	Because of that unfinished business – –
	which I have been putting off.
	However, what exactly is it that is unfinished?
GALINA	Yes, that's it. That's it, Vivian.
	You are a true friend. I always thought you were.
	It was painful for me to broach this subject.
	I came to you this morning because during the night
	I came to the realization that I myself
	have some unfinished business.
	But please don't imagine I can tell you any particulars.

43

	An extreme restlessness came over me.
	I said yes to it. Do you know what I mean by that?
VIVIAN	Yes, I believe I do.
	Because I usually say no.
	When uncomfortable doubts rise up in me
	I sweep them under the carpet.
	I'm afraid I've made a bit of a habit of that.
	But tell me, have you arrived at some conclusion about this?
	During the night, of all things?
GALINA	'Fraid so. No, not afraid so.
	I've decided to take the bull by the horns.
	Or put it this way: I half decided,
	Then I decided to talk to you.
VIVIAN	I'm glad you did.
	Uncomfortable as it makes me feel,
	I'm glad you did.
	If there's anyone I can admit this to, it's you, Galina.
	Most people I know are not plagued by doubts.
	At least that's what they would say.
	So I say fine, let them get on with it.
	They certainly wouldn't want to know about mine.
GALINA	But we blame ourselves a little, for harbouring doubts,
	Don't we. That layer of hypocrisy that weighs
	Down on the world is so – so thick – and heavy.
VIVIAN	Is it hypocrisy? Or is it just fear?
GALINA	The hypocrisy is the misguided way of dealing with the fear.
	I feel confident in saying that because I describe my own.
	But Vivian, I have to tell you,
	You know I've never been religious,
	I have avoided the very notion of a god
	Or of any spirit that reaches into us
	But I have to tell you, I heard this voice,

During the night, it was terrible at first,
It forced me to listen, told me I had no choice,
Not if I wanted to live. I feel foolish saying this to you,
I certainly could not confide in anyone else.
It made me feel that I was chosen for some task,
It would have to do with a renewal of sorts,
A new human being that was developing –
And I would be involved in letting others know about it.
That would be my contribution.
What do you think, am I going crazy?
Perhaps its very wrong of me to talk about this,
To involve anyone in the uncertainty I feel.
And yet it's more a certainty than an uncertainty,
Because I was presented with an undeniable claim
That was made on me, on my time, my awareness.
Please say something now. I feel very exposed.

VIVIAN   You have certainly had an experience, Galina.
Oh dear, look, you're trembling.
I have never seen you like this.
Did this voice identify itself?

GALINA   No, I don't think so. It was all a case of:
'I am doing something to you, the meaning of which
Will in time become plain to you,
And it has to do with a new way to be.'

VIVIAN   Were you told to perform some particular task?

GALINA   No, not as such. A definite spiritual presence
Advised me strongly to take account of it
And to consider myself somehow renewed,
But for the purpose of making this clear to others.
I wish I could say I'm willing, Vivian, but I'm not.
All my life I have insisted on understanding,
On knowing ahead of time what I was doing,
And here I'm to act in blind faith,

In a direction I can't make out,
For a reason with which I can't identify.

VIVIAN   It must be awful! How you are bound to feel.
But what if it's faith and not blind faith?
After all, in comparison to what we call reason,
Faith is blind. We assent to something that
Impresses us inwardly, that we believe because
We can't doubt it. I would certainly encourage you
To believe what you experienced.
But believe it as a whole human being,
Not as someone who wants some sign of the truth.
This might in fact be your predicament, that you
Look for a sign that the truth is true and not false.
This may, after all, be the first time that you've
Actually experience the physical truth.
And you experienced it as a commanding voice.
I believe you have reason to be grateful, Galina.
I should tell you too that what you say does
Not in the least frighten me. My inner security
Is not disturbed but confirmed.

GALINA   Oh if you knew how it helps me to hear that, Vivian!
I have never in my life shrugged off responsibility,
So if this is in truth something that is meant for me
Then I will not turn aside from it.
And it would make sense, wouldn't it, if
Time was required, a lot of time, before a person
could feel comfortable with something like this.
It would have to sink in properly.
And that's what your are helping me with,
You wonderful man. You are not turning away.

VIVIAN   I want you to be quite sure of me, Galina.
If good spirit has singled you out for something,
Then you are very fortunate indeed –

46

As are we who know you.

GALINA   Good spirit? Is that something you know?

VIVIAN   It's how I think of god.

GALINA   You call it god? All I know of god is hypocrisy,
Sentimentality, hysteria, that is what I have come to
Associate with the concept 'God'.

VIVIAN   All the same, the reality of it is good spirit.
I have all my life called it that.
Good spirit. We are always influenced by good spirit.
More or less. To the degree that we can … well …
Digest, I suppose. But it helps to cooperate.
I myself, you see, have never been asked to make any
Special effort in the way of my believing.
But here, the way you confide in me, the way you
Trust me with all this information,
This does make me responsible, in a new way,
And I feel honoured to be asked to bear that responsibility.

GALINA   Will we keep in touch about this?
Please say yes.

VIVIAN   Yes, yes, for sure, Galina. Have no doubt about that.

GALINA   I have come to you in the middle of the night
And you opened the door to me.
Now I fell comforted and I will go again.
I may be able to sleep a while.

VIVIAN   I hope you will. You feel alright about driving back home?

GALINA   Yes, very much so, now. Thank you again.
My friend. My true friend.

GALINA   *(leaves)*

VIVIAN   What a great honour it is to be especially touched by god.
I must admit I am jealous – just a little.

47

However I'm involved, and that means much.

Scene 3

*(**Galina**, **Ted**, later **Lorraine**)*
at Galina's apartment)

GALINA   I need knowledge. More and more knowledge.
Where, oh where would we be without it!
Happily nowadays the likes of me can work from home.
I thought I'd start at the bottom, at the
Elementary grass roots level,
The place where genius goes, for its strength.
It used to be Eros, then Eros turned into sex
And even genius burnt itself out.
Well, thank goodness we can do better nowadays.
So I invited a member of the Chorus over,
For a little discussion, if he's willing.
He should arrive any time now.
It was the way he once said:
"This is about to turn into a soap opera"
That drew my attention to him.
He insisted the discussion would have to be formal
And that's fine by me. As a matter of fact
I would be smart to prefer that.
What I want is respect, not mateyness.

(the doorbell rings)

Here we go. Right on time.
Now let me see what I can find out.

(walks to door to let Tim in)

GALINA   Come in. Please. Thanks for coming right away.
You're the one that's referred to as M1, is that right?

48

TED	That's my moniker.
GALINA	And under ordinary circumstances – Ted, is that right?
TED	Let's not get the two mixed up. I'm a modern individual and I pride myself on being dual – on appearing as two halves.
GALINA	A most unusual sense of pride.
TED	So what's it all about? I realize that we lot are at your disposal But I was going to do something else today.
GALINA	Oh don't be angry. I know I'm taking advantage of you. Maybe I'll give you a nice lunch, how about that? In the meanwhile I need to run something past you. I dare say you're familiar with the works of Shakespeare,
TED	Marginally. Don't ask me to identify quotations.
GALINA	And Nietzsche?
TED	Never heard of him.
GALINA	What about Paul of Tarsus, Saint Paul, as he's called by some believers? Are you a believer?
TED	No on both counts. I believe I'm here on earth to get on as well as I'm able until I die. That's the extent of it.
GALINA	Well, that's perfectly workable, I'm sure. It means you are free of certain prejudices. It means that to me any-how. Our civilization has just gone through one of the worst upheavals on record. You weren't born at the time but you carry the after-effects in your genes. For example if I said: 'birthright', what would you say?

TED	I'd say you have to be more specific. The devil do I care, that's my immediate response, off the cuff, like.
GALINA	Thank you for being honest, that's most important for me.
TED	No skin off my back.
GALINA	Next I need to know how many of your kind, do you suppose, are delighted by pain inflicted on others?
TED	I have to get out my phone. Here, one moment – (types) – here it is. The answer you require is Multitude. What does it mean?
GALINA	Do you like using those machines?
TED	Wouldn't be without it. Look how fast I could answer your question.
GALINA	Next. As a cross section, how do you relate the angelic beings to the various constellations of the heavenly stars – I mean if required to do so by an examiner, for example, when you apply for some paid position at a state-controlled industrial site?
TED	Ah, now that is the sort of question I like. It's my bread and butter. I like to dine out on that sort. Mind you, I wasn't expecting to hear it from the likes of you. My guess is you're a spy.
GALINA	Got it in one. I spy for The cosmic world order.
TED	Run that past me again?
GALINA	The cosmic world order. It's on the cards. I'm one of the few who are dealing. I found out only a week ago.
TED	Well! Indeed! Hat's off! In that case: I relate to those angelic beings by entertaining every wit and whim they

50

throw my way. They are, as it were, the only hold on reality that I've got. The likes of me ain't got much of that sort, if you know what I mean. You wouldn't want to be hard on me now?

GALINA   Oh gracious me! Furthest thing from my mind, Ted.

TED   Sorry Ma'm, could we keep it formal? M1, if you don't mind.

GALINA   Ah, I see. By the way, were you the male who was present when Vivian and I met again, some days ago?

TED   That's me, Ma'm.

GALINA   I thought so.
It occurred to me at the time to ask about you.
Your comments were frivolous. What makes you up?

TED   Sorry?

GALINA   Your matter. The matter of which you are composed.
You must have some notion?
It would help me to relate to you.

TED   Ah, I see what you mean.

Five percent hello-how-do-you-do, which is bright,
and ninety-five dark.
Dark matter and dark energy.
Slim difference between them.

GALINA   Remarkable that you should be so clued in.
Is dark matter not evil? I mean tantamount to evil?

TED   It is, Ma'm, yes. It would be wrong of me to deny it.

GALINA   So how do you cope?

TED   Why it's simple. The evil you don't resist
leaves you in peace.
It's negative, you see.

51

	If you push against it, which I don't advise, it pushes back – Sometimes much harder, oh yes; then there's trouble.
GALINA	So that goes for you as much as for me?
TED	That part, yes. Indeed yes.
GALINA	So under certain circumstances you would kill, am I right?
TED	I would not be able to stop myself, Ma'm. Fifteen percent is readily overruled.
GALINA	And right now you draw on those fifteen percent?
TED	I do, Ma'm, yes. You and I seem to get along fine.
GALINA	Well, I am very much obliged to you. I have learned a great deal; In fact more than I hoped to be able to manage today. By the way, who was the female on that day when you saw me the first time?
TED	That was F1; or Lorraine, Ma'm. She was most impressed by the account you gave of yourself.
GALINA	Was she indeed! I wonder would you be able to put me in touch with her, so that I can ask her …
TED	By snapping my fingers, Ma'm.
GALINA	Are you serious?
TED	(snaps his fingers – **Lorraine** appears)
LORRAINE	Yes Ted. Good to hear from you. And what are we up to today?
TED	This good lady, Galina by name, wants to speak with you.
LORRAINE	That's what we're here for. Hello to you. I've seen you before, last Wednesday, Ted and I were both there.

TED	Lorraine!
LORRAINE	Oh! Is this formal? It is, isn't it. I should have noticed.
GALINA	No, it's my fault. I have not yet taken the opportunity to explain what I have in mind. A few simple questions? Woman to female? Nothing personal, obviously.
LORRAINE	Shoot. No problem.
GALINA	The material make-up of the female, that's what interests me. Now M1 here spoke of ninety-five percent dark matter. When you push, he said, it pushes back.
LORRAINE	Oh yes. Exactly. We're all millionaires in that department. It's not until we go informal and you give us our names that there's any difference between us – between the females and the males. Cut from the same elemental cloth, so to speak. I have never been asked that. It feels great to be able to respond. Ask another.
GALINA	Are we talking unisex here too?
ANNIE	Of course. And how! Hence the fireworks. Don't you get involved now.
GALINA	Why not?
LORRAINE	You'd lose you capital. For sure. You'd end up weaving baskets and crocheting stars. It's alright for the likes of us because we have nothing to lose. We rise out of the 'primordial' and sink down into it again and no harm done.
TED	However those ninety-five percent have their uses.
LORRAINE	You shut up now! This is my own ten minutes in the light.

TED	Your tone leaves something to be desired.
LORRAINE	You know what you can do with 'your tone'!
TED	Just you turn around and I'll know where to put it!
GALINA	Folks! Folks! Please, let's stay calm.
LORRAINE	And you know what you can do with your 'folks'! We ain't folks, alright? Folks is laptop decoration. Folks is your horse-shite on the fetlock, Rust on the flintlock, lice on he hair-lock.
TED	You're running over at the mouth, Lorraine. Cut it. You're forgetting who's here.
GALINA	Well look, you two, I have what I need and I certainly don't wish to inconvenience you. You must have important business elsewhere.

*(**Ted** and **Lorraine** were already leaving, arguing)*

I think that was worth it. I had to start somewhere.
I am not, after all, involved in a simple-minded reformation.
Also, no doubt, the cosmic reality insists on its
Own rate of growth.
Now I can go <u>out</u> for my lunch.

———

Scene 4

*(**Vivian** and **Uncle Werner,** later **Carl,** in Vivian's apartment)*

UNCLE W.	Oh I was pleased to pop over. Didn't realize you live so close.
VIVIAN	I've been meaning to get in touch since last Wednesday. In the meantime I spoke to Galina. Are you well, Uncle Werner? That's the first thing. What I'm going to say to you will Take a bit of bearing up under, if you know what I mean.

54

	Oh nothing drastic, don't worry,
	Merely out of the ordinary, and let's face it,
	We're none of us quite ready to deal with that, are we,
	I mean at the drop of a hat,
	What with this normalization phase of the world.
UNCLE W.	Oh quite. Normalization. I give in to it, don't you know.
	Once you begin to resist normalization
	You are on your way to the hoosegow.
	(*the doorbell*)
	There's your bell – ?
VIVIAN	I'm not expecting anyone.
	(*goes to door to let in **Carl***)
	Look who it is!
	It's Carl, isn't it? Welcome!
CARL	Please, sir, if you don't mind: M2.
	This is work. I am merely functional.
	I bring a message, as you might expect.
	(*to **Uncle Werner***) Hello, sir.
UNCLE W.	(*nods*)
VIVIAN	So what have you to tell us, M2?
CARL	Message from our drama director, namely Trevor, sir.
	Maintains he would appreciate us to foregather.
	That's clumsy. Has it in mind we might all
	Traipse to the theatre to continue with what he calls
	Performance practice. Investiture practice too.
	It seems the costumes are ready and willing, sir,
	So the man Trevor sees fit to call us to the fold,
	And one day earlier than planned.
	That's my message, sir, front to back and well smoothed.
VIVIAN	Complete with buttons, M2. Delightful.
	Now here's my response, which you may be

Kind enough to take to Trevor.
Not only is my day today fully planned,
But tomorrow too, so I shall not attend his playacting
Until Friday at the earliest.
Uncle Werner, you must give your own answer.

UNCLE W.   Indeed. It's as follows – and I shall refashion it
Specifically for your messenger ears, M2,
As soon as I have conversed with Sir Clough.
Our conversation – will it be private, Vivian?

VIVIAN   It will not be understood, let me put it that way.

UNCLE W.   Then stay by all means, M2, until Sir Clough and I
Have come to terms here.
Take a seat, please. *(Carl sits down)*

VIVIAN   Indeed we may welcome your input, M2.
Wait until you hear.
A very good friend of ours, whom I will not name
But Uncle Werner will know whom I mean,
Has experienced a spiritual visitation. Oh dear,
That is a clumsy word for it; evidently it
Embarrasses me to speak of it,
However speak of it we must.
Her eyes have been opened to the other side
And her ears have perceived –
Not entirely willingly, I may add –
The most astonishing – for her – information.
It concerns us. We are friends.

UNCLE W.   Has she seen a vision or heard a voice – or both?

VIVIAN   Mostly the latter, I believe.
No, altogether the latter.

UNCLE W.   I see. It's a shocking thing.
Has she become deranged by it?

VIVIAN	No. No. She is a mature woman, as you know, And she has begun to make sense of it. Also she has asked me to inform her friends here. To let them know that if she seems distant, It is because – well, because she is rather busy.
CARL	If I may speak, sir, this is nothing, To me it happens once a week, on average. I hear voices and am given messages, However the gist of it falls apart upon examination. You must advise this lady to put it out of her mind.
VIVIAN	Ah, thank you for that, Carl. However she has confided in me and she assures me An appreciable burden has been placed upon her And she carries it willingly. That is how she puts it. Something about a grave responsibility, Especially on behalf of the afflicted among us.
UNCLE W.	The afflicted! I say, that is good news. Dare we hope it relates to the Evolution for which so many of us are longing? Has that word come up, by any chance?
CARL	In other words, is she a Darwinist?
VIVIAN	No, M2. Not that sort of evolution. I know what Uncle Werner means. He means the very fruition of humanity. The expression of human being of itself as divine. He means the very unfolding of human beings themselves As complete, perfect and whole, like their maker.
CARL	I'm afraid that's beyond me, sir.
VIVIAN	I imagined it might be. However do continue to listen, because What we say will affect you. Yes it will.

(turning to Uncle Werner)

In answer to your question now, Uncle Werner,
Yes indeed, we may hope.
As we know, mostly from the arcana, I dare say,
The feminine input is to be as crucial as the masculine.
We may have a precious example of it here.
Galina has 'her head screwed on', we may
Take that for granted. What she will appreciate is
Our understanding, that's the long and the short of it.

UNCLE W.   Has she given you confidences?

VIVIAN   She says we must be on our guard, principally against
Influences from the direction of our 'amour propre',
That is our love of self, M2; more specifically our
Selfish affection. I must admit
I know all too well what she means by that.
I am fond of <u>you</u>, why will <u>you</u> not be fond of <u>me</u>,
That sort of thing. It runs amazingly deep.
I recall, once in the Canadian Rockies,
Standing directly above the location where
The glacial water from Lake McArthur escapes
Underground, roars, as it were, under one's feet,
And I thought to myself, at the time,
Some day this will come in handy, as a vivid image.
So we need to make room for that.

UNCLE W.   And I dare say those of our own household
Will therefore be our worst enemies at times.
Can you recall anything else from her?

VIVIAN   Let me see. She spoke of the importance of
Respect for the other gender, as if that, too,
Might present a major hindrance to the
Smooth transition – the smoothness being
Essentially theoretical, she stressed that, I recall.

58

UNCLE W.   In other words we are bound to react
           To every encouragement to growth along the way.
           (to M2) You are beginning to fidget, M2.
           If this causes you stress, do try to take that
           As a telling example of what we mean here.
           The stress is a sign that you have what it takes
           To make a move forward in the direction of –
           In your case – the popular amendment.
           Would you agree, Vivian, that
           Even in the case of the unenlightened
           There is opportunity for – for rectification, shall we say?

VIVIAN   Now this may be where you come in, Uncle Werner.
           It would not surprise me if you were to come up with
           A special giftedness in this direction.
           I have noticed how you relate to M2.
           What say you, M2?
           Which is the voice you hear most clearly?
           Uncle Werner's voice or mine?

CARL   The former sir, if I may make bold to say so.

VIVIAN   *(to Uncle Werner)* There you go. What did I say!
           You may have your work cut out for you
           In relation to what you continue to make out from
           Galina's direction.

CARL   It's getting the better of me, sirs.
           I can no longer sit still.
           My legs are threatening to strike out on their own
           And my tongue's in a fury to wag to its heart's content.
           I leave. I return to our dramatic director.
           May I pass on the message that
           You too, Uncle Werner, will be available,
           For a further exercise of the art, in two days' time?

VIVIAN   Bless you, M2. We appreciated your company. Be well.

59

(**M2** *bows out*)

Now that has served us as a sufficient demonstration
At least of the effectiveness of human evolution
In the direction of the popular realm.
Of course, as usual, it's the individual case that will tell.

UNCLE W.   This is all very exciting! And most relevant to our time.
We must take care to clothe it in the
Right sort of language. And prepare for being charged
With obscurantism. All in a day's work.

VIVIAN   Not to forget humour. No evolution without humour.
Above all let's not try to present Galina's originality as
'THE TRUTH', you know, in capital letters.
She would be the last to wish that.
However I strongly feel that her work should be
Facilitated – if that's the right word.

UNCLE W.   No doubt she will write?

VIVIAN   I believe she has made a start.

UNCLE W.   Well, excellent. Now here's a question:
What about Trevor? We are both well aware
Of his various attempts to expand the histrionic art
Over the total realm of human awareness.
'Let the voice and the eye marry', that sort of thing.
I wonder, is he wrong? What do you suppose?

VIVIAN   Oh dear yes! Well do I know what you're driving at!
And is anything more relevant nowadays in our world
Than the feminine influence?

UNCLE W.   The rights of the female to choose to become feminine,
Yes, and yes again! The very definition of what it means
To be a woman rather than 'a female'!
This is pushing through along
                every conceivable walk of life.

By any and all means, I say,
                let knowledge and understanding
Be brought to bear on these topics, and issues;
In a word, on these crises.
After all, looking around, we are being
Presented with one gender-related crisis after the other.

VIVIAN   And not just in our neck of the woods.

UNCLE W.   Oh indeed! Africa, the Middle East, Asia, South America.
               And how sadly so much of it peters out, or goes wrong!

VIVIAN   For the lack of the sort of understanding which, perhaps,
               Our Galina will help to supply.

UNCLE W.   How appropriate that she was a dancer!

———————

Act III

Scene 1

(Trish, Alphonse, Miriam, Trevor, Galina,
Lorraine, Frank.** Later **Annie, Rita, Carl** and **Ted**)

MIRIAM   So how was my baby this morning?

TRISH   She had a perfect night's sleep, and so did we, you'll be
            glad to know. Before we put her to bed we encouraged
            her to talk about you and she did that. She has decided
            already that she has a daddy now but two mummies,
            which makes her special.

MIRIAM   Oh I'm so glad! It has been tricky for me, all week, well
            obviously, what did I expect, and I balance that against
            not worrying about what happens at that kindergarten
            cum holding centre, against having to rush in the
            morning to take her there and then picking her up after
            work when I'm dog tired and can't really spend any
            pleasant time with her at all. And all it comes down to is
            that we're all bigger than our circumstances,
            isn't that right?

ALPHONSE   Yes, especially the legal circumstances.

MIRIAM   How do you mean?

ALPHONSE   Well, as if it really mattered to a child – I mean unless
            you drummed it in to her – who is her so-called legal
            guardian. What she cares about is how she is being
            treated, from one day to the next. There is sentimental
            love, and possessive love and egotistic love, and really
            there should never be any more of those than let's us
            notice what we're up to after ten seconds.

TRISH   Lorraine is good with her, Miriam. Did you know that?

62

MIRIAM   Oh, is that right, Lorraine? Have you taken a shine to my baby?

LORRAINE   She's not a baby any more, for God's sake, Miriam. She's nearly two. Stop calling her a baby.
            It's sickening.

MIRIAM   Oh, excuse me! Actually I was only playing. What are babies, after all, unless they're somebody else's?

ALPHONSE   No one can really answer that question until they have once held a newly-born baby, and automatically rocked it in their arms.

MIRIAM   You're right, of course. The rest is lies to make up for impatience and anger.

ALPHONSE   And rage. Read the newspapers. Babies are murdered.

LORRAINE   That's perfectly believable.

TREVOR   (enters) That's great, folks. That's in the can.
            A little short on substance but …

ALPHONSE   No! Surely not, Trevor.
            That seemed perfectly genuine to me.
            I nearly forgot that I was not the father.

TREVOR   Well, you see, you shouldn't forget that in fact you're not the real father. It's this business of becoming submerged in your role. Wear your figure – your character, as it used to be called – the way you wear your face. There's the mature face and there's the immature face. Either you use it or it abuses you. Either it gives you away or you hand it over.

ALPHONSE   So give us a working definition of what you mean by substance, Trevor.

TREVOR   First of all, as I say so often, you keep the

63

audience in mind. Or put it this way: You don't forget
that what you say and do is said and done for others,
not for your ego. That's the essence of it, as I see it.
But I would expect all of you to be in the possession of
your own version of that. The egotistic performance
fascinates, we all know that, but fascination is magic
and without substance. Those who come to our plays
have a right to look for substance. If they want to be
thrilled and excited and – in other words – alienated
from their questionable self for a brief period,
there are lots of places where they can get that.

LORRAINE   You need bums in seats, don't you, Trevor?

TREVOR   You never, ever try to facilitate that, Lorraine.
It's a thing that happens, one way or the other.
Art is specifically for human beings. I grant you we're
short on precedents. We make up for that
with functional insight and contemporary talent.
    (**Galina** *enters, with* **Frank** *in train*)
Galina! For goodness sake! Where've <u>you</u> been?
You look bushed. Anything wrong?

GALINA   No, not at all. I was sitting out in the hall,
as a member of the audience, as it were.
Young Frank here spotted me. I feel so heavy, Trevor.
I feel like I have the weight of the earth on my
shoulders. But listen – your performance. Very nice.
That's what persuaded me to join you on the stage.
What if I can shed some of my weight up there, I thought.
No, really, it will take me a little while to figure out
what's going on with me.

TREVOR   Yes, well, I heard that you had a vision, or a dream;
I've heard several stories. Maybe that's what is pressing
down on you. Lorraine, please get Galina a cup of coffee.

GALINA	No, no coffee, please. It would wreck what little nerve I have left. Thank you anyway, Trevor. If I could just be with you all a little. Would you mind awfully? I believe it would do me good. Help me to come out of my self. Hello Patricia, Alphonse, F1.
LORRAINE	It's Lorraine, please.
GALINA	Sorry. I still don't understand why and when it changes. No, don't explain. I wouldn't be able to take it in. You know what I'd like most of all? If I could participate in your play for a scene or two. No, just one scene, that would fix me up, I'm sure.
TRISH	Why don't you play <u>my</u> part for a while, Galina? I'll stand by and watch. Would you like that?
GALINA	Oh splendid. Let's get started. I have your blessing, Trevor?
TREVOR	Absolutely. Take it from where Lorraine says: That's perfectly believable, after Alphonse has mentioned the murder of babies. You'll find your way in, Galina. *(he leaves the stage)*
ALPHONSE	And rage. Read the newspapers. Babies are murdered.
LORRAINE	That's perfectly believable. A maiden aunt of mine did just that. Mind you, she was known for her shaky temperament.
GALINA	She must have gone through hell afterwards.
LORRAINE	I'm afraid she's still in it. Nobody can come up with the help she needs to be able to face what she did.
ALPHONSE	We'll have to watch our step, Trish. When the chips are down we'll depend on you, Miriam, to help us see it through.

LORRAINE	Mind you, all those trials come our way for a specific purpose. There's a lot to be said for the affected individual buckling down to … you know … to the burden in hand. You and I, Alphonse, should always tackle everything together first, before we go elsewhere for help, don't you think? Oh no … I can't do it. So sorry. Quick, help me, someone.
TREVOR	(*comes on*) Frank, catch her! (*they help the semi-conscious Galina into an easy-chair.*) Get some cold water, someone. We don't have any spirits, do we? No. If she rests, maybe. Let's all wish her well. That's most important. Let's be with her in spirit. Here, group around. She's trying to speak.
GALINA	If we, in the world as it is now, could see the world as it will soon be, we would say: How boring! And when those in that world look back at what we called our world they will say: How horrible! Oh, if I could sleep a little now. I do apologize for being a burden to you.
TREVOR	Not at all, Galina. Be at ease. Look, here, Frank has brought you some water. Take a sip or two, for form's sake. You do lack form and that's the truth.
GALINA	(*drinks*) I have heard the voice of god and it has shocked me out of my system. Now I have to experiment. Everything that was mine, now I have to hand it over. With every fibre of my being I have to register the new life now. In addition to that, as I dare say you have noticed, I am not allowed to hide away and hug my predicament to myself instead of showing my good fortune. Thank you for letting me speak. If I cannot speak I collapse within myself. The new life –

that is what it's about – what is at stake. If we do not
make room for it within ourselves, it makes space for
itself inside us and that must seem like death to us then.
And the process from that death to life is unimaginable.
It forces so many of us to the sidelines –
even right off the stage. And that is so sad then,
because we will always know, when we look at
those who fall away, that it might have been otherwise.
However it is a sadness that allows us to explore –
to explore further reaches and terrains, further tracts of
thought and emotion, of body and mind, of spirit and
flesh – all to become one. All to become one.
(*she falls asleep*)

TREVOR   There let her sleep for a while. We will stay nearby.
Call Annie and Rita. Carl and Ted. Let them all help.
What we do for Galina we do for all of us.

(***Annie**, **Rita**, **Carl** and **Ted** come on stage. **Trevor**
quietly informs them of what is required. In the end **Galina**,
asleep in her chair, is surrounded by the rest of the cast who
are seated on the floor, each in silent meditation*)

Scene 2
*(same as previous – soft musical sounds
accompany the speaking voice)*

VOICE   Here we have the right beginning
Of the human-natural scene.
No more thought of sexy sinning.

No more thought dismembers feeling,
No more love that builds on thought
While the modern head is reeling.

67

Gentle female-male inclining,
Children playing while they grow,
Love community defining.

*(a veiled figure, **Galina's spirit**, appears to step out of Galina's chair, moves among the seated figures and touches each carefully on the shoulder, but never on the head.)*

When good spirit moves within them,
Those who tremble and are lively
Let humanity begin them.

Others only know conjecture
On the outside of the world
And at times they need a lecture.

Not for us to point the finger
To emancipate the spirits
Where they practice, where they linger.

Ours now but to wisely know
Time no longer is advancing
While we understand and grow.

*(the **music** stops – the **spirit** returns to whence it came – now all the figures on the stage, including **Galina**, stand up and move about.)*

GALINA   Thank you so much, all of you, for helping me.
I actually knew I was depending on you.
At the same time I had this wonderful dream.

TRISH   Oh, so did I!

LORRAINE   Me too! Wow!

TREVOR   Did we all dream? Yes? That's fascinating. I imagined –
Or did I imagine it? – I seemed to be
drifting through space and it pleased me no end,
but then I came down to earth

and the pleasure, well, it was so substantial, so that
I realized gravity was like being in love with the earth.
I suppose that sounds ridiculous.

RITA   Wait till you hear what I dreamt. All my friends and I
were involved in a complicated dance and no matter
how much we concentrated, things went wrong, we
bumped into one another and stepped on each other's
feet – until someone suggested we should forget entirely
about the routine we were trying to learn. Suddenly,
as soon as we did that, we danced in unison,
everything fitted beautifully.

TED   I believe I was one of your friends, Rita.

ANNIE   Yes, so was I, I actually fell headlong one time, does anyone
else recall that? No? That's extraordinary.

CARL   Frank, you were there. I corrected your movements
several times, didn't I, I mean before it all turned out well.

FRANK   I don't recall that, Carl, but the mistakes I made
infuriated me. Then, as soon as we all agreed to do our
own thing, I was amazed how well you danced.
And I was no longer conscious of myself. How well I
remember that now!

ALPHONSE I have to tell you that I dreamt nothing at all,
however I was aware of Galina's spirit moving among us
and touching us. I could not have spoken, I probably
wouldn't have been able to move if I had tried, but I only
observed. In the meantime I knew – yes, it was knowledge –
that it was up to me to let you all know what went on
in reality. The spirit of Galina – don't ask me to describe it.
A human shape. Were you aware of that, Galina?

GALINA   No. Definitely not. I believe you completely, by the way,
when you describe what you saw, Alphonse.

No, I merely existed – though in perfect self-awareness.
My dream was more like a realization of myself.
Here and now, I thought – yes, I thought! –
I am becoming who I am. By the way, this took
an eternity of time. I understood eternity.
I was reminded of the corner stone being put in place –
in my case. From now on I would know what was
up to me to accomplish during the rest of my life on earth.
Certainty, yes. May I put it like this? I received the gift of
certainty. Oh you are all so good to listen to me. Am I
rambling? No, I know I'm not. I even heard Trevor say
that you would all stand by me –

LORRAINE Which was when we all sat down?
(laughter)

GALINA Indeed! And you said, Trevor – at least what I heard was –
What we do for Galina we do for us all.
Did you really say that?

TREVOR Whatever I said, that was certainly my meaning.
I considered even then that there was a special
blessing on you, and we may all be sure of that now.
I believe the emphasis ought to be on what we
learn from you – not so much from what you say
but from your presence among us. Especially from that,
but basically from your being around, from the fact that
you exist. I don't feel that this brings on my ego at all.
What I feel is gratitude.

ALPHONSE Well said. Well spoken, Trevor. I can vouch for this
gratitude. I feel it too. It believe it extends over
all of us here. How long this will stay alive in us
I can't say, but we should be able to fall back on it
at a time of a shortage of confidence.

TRISH Yes, we were all involved in this, that is what is so

70

marvellous. I guess your spirit, Galina, will always be
available to us.

GALINA   And so will yours be available to me. Do you know
what it was? It was not my spirit at all, strictly speaking.
It was the communal spirit. It was the spirit that
draws us all to a common humanity.
The association with me was happenstance.
There we have it. We are all in the clear.
Now it's time for me to go home and
write a few things down. Yes, I have begun to take my
writing seriously. Will you see me out to my car, Trevor,
please? I have hung my coat in the hall.
*(**Trevor** and **Galina** leave,*
the others wave to Galina, who responds)

Scene 3

*(**Vivian** and **Uncle Werner**)*

VIVIAN   Oh yes, Galina has been in touch.
I confess, Uncle Werner, that her presence,
I mean near me, unnerves me now, can you believe that?
No, even on the telephone, where I heard from her last –
and isn't it amazing how we can speak of
being somewhere with someone, albeit on the telephone? –
It quite frightened me when I noticed how I began to
tremble, to dither in my speech, to become
disorganised in my thought. My very thought processes
became so jumbled that I repeated
phrases and left out crucial pronouns
or raised and lowered my voice at
totally inappropriate places.

UNCLE W.   Oh my! Why had she called you? Or had you called her?

VIVIAN	Yes, the latter. I merely wanted to know how she was getting on. I must tell you that it turned into an invasion of my private life, no less.
UNCLE W.	You're joking! Galina! The epitome of tact?
VIVIAN	Oh pardon me, that was not her intention, merely how I reacted. I would say: even her tone of voice – not what she said but something that came along with it, like steel needles and iron filings. And the point is, I was at the mercy of it. I could no more have said to her: Please do not do this to me! or have asked her what she meant by making me feel like this, than I could ask you right now why you constantly gnash your teeth. The fact is, you don't and you know that.
UNCLE W.	Aha, that certainly clarifies it for me. If I were a psychoanalyst I would zero in on your brain functions and get you to describe how you feel if I clap my hands or breath down you neck.
VIVIAN	Oh please don't make fun of me. I am fond of Galina.
UNCLE W.	Well, there you have it. That explains it all. Better, it opens doors for you.
VIVIAN	Now what could you possibly mean by that, Uncle?
UNCLE W.	First or all, what business have you being fond of Galina? Indeed being fond of anyone? It's a disease. Not until it's pointed out to us of course. I myself have been affected, I assure you. Now the object – yes the object – of your fondness seems uncommonly harsh. Poor you. I commiserate, to be sure. However let the truth prevail. If we cannot speak the truth on the stage we may as well

72

fold up our personalities. Take it from me then, Vivian,
much as I respect you and honour your distinctive
individuality, we are only allowed to become
fond of one another for the distinct purpose of
learning how to love. Take it as an invitation.

VIVIAN   I should love Galina?

UNCLE W.   Evidently.

VIVIAN   But is love not an emotional extension of fondness?
Perhaps even the passionate shape of fondness?

UNCLE W.   No, my friend. Indeed not. If I may make so bold as to
instruct you: Fondness is the seed that must die
so that love may flourish. Of course I mean
intentional love, the good will of the body and the brain
in unison. The question is: Are you the man?
Or, if you like, are you man enough?

VIVIAN   Oh sweet Jesus, what are you up to, Uncle!
Am I to continue to listen to you?

UNCLE W.   If you wish. It's not obligatory. I have other things to do.

VIVIAN   I say, you have wiped me out, haven't you.
This makes me wonder am I still the human being I was
ten minutes ago. I believe I shall go into decline for a spell.
If there were whisky in the house I would reach for it.
I cannot just run off and leave you standing there.
We are friends, are we not?

UNCLE W.   I concentrate on doing what is best for us.
Not for me but for us.
I find myself joining you in your vastation.
Gratitude overwhelms me.
Yes, evidently we are great friends.
Might I venture to guess that you and I are
enjoying the good fortune of a moment of

evolutionary growth. Best not to time it.

VIVIAN   Shall I remain passive?

UNCLE W.   Only until you begin to fidget, to reach for the whiskey,
to turn on the mass-media – or to hanker for euthanasia.
Stick it out until then, if you would please.
And please, do not hold it against me
that I know what I am talking about.

VIVIAN   Might we make a little light conversation in the meantime?
While death takes its toll?

UNCLE W.   Up to you.

VIVIAN   The weather has been fine. I shall holiday in Bali this time.

UNCLE W.   Splendid! Bali. Peaceful – picturesque, from what I recall.

VIVIAN   A little more. There's a chap in town who charges
unconscionable sums for arranging hiking tours through
the Himalayas, the Balkans, adventures in Patagonia,
bathing holidays near the Dead Sea. No, that will do me.
I am about to exert myself – if only I can still find myself.
Yes, I can. Elsewhere, mind you. The anxiety, thankfully,
has passed. Dear me, I have been unmanned and
rediscovered myself. Not the sort of thing one ever
anticipates or expects to bump into
just around the next corner.

UNCLE W.   Well, good for you. Indeed good for us.
What are friends for, eh?

VIVIAN   I notice a distinct sensation of masculinity.
Due to a spiritual discipline, to be sure.
Thank you ever so much for your help. Did you have to
ask for courage before you told me the truth?

UNCLE W.   I did, Vivian. You can say that again. One always risks
losing the better friend one may gain by clinging to the

lesser friend one still has.

VIVIAN   So are you quite familiar with speaking the truth?
             Do you do it often?

UNCLE W.   Rarely on the stage.

VIVIAN   Why so?

UNCLE W.   To be honest, I am too much of a coward.

VIVIAN   Would now be the time for a drink?

UNCLE W.   Yes! Yes! Ha! If not now, when, eh?
             (*Vivian pours. They toast each other*)

VIVIAN   To the truth!

UNCLE W.   To the truth!

_____

Act IV

Scene 1

*(all the **players** on stage – **Trevor** and **Tim** in centre, **the rest** on the outskirts)*

TREVOR   (*to audience*) We skip a few years, I hope no one objects.
Time is of the essence, so we have to keep on top of it.
Personally, in my private life – little of it as I have left,
and no wonder, when you consider how creativity gradually
wipes the borderlines between the two – as I say,
in my private life …

TRISH   Stick to the point, Trevor!

TREVOR   What? Oh, thank you, Trish. I was never much good at
speaking directly to an audience. It draws the
soul from me. Anyway, several years have flown,
Trish and Alphonse have returned from Peru with their
nearly grown-up youngster – you remember Tim, he was
adopted by them, Miriam's child initially, now that was
an interesting story, they were ….

ALPHONSE   Trevor, the audience itself hasn't been away fifteen years!
I believe we can take for granted they'll be able to recall
most of this.

TREVOR   Sure. Sure. I just like to fill in some bits and pieces.

TRISH   Why not let Tim speak for himself?

TREVOR   Oh! Has he arrived? Good. I wasn't aware. Nobody
tells me anything anymore. Art is gobbling up life
and we poor players may strut and fret all we like,
eventually we give up the ghost. Very well then,
bring on Tim, if he's ready.
I'm expecting big things from him.
Aren't we all!

TIM   *(led on by **Alphonse**, who whispers something into his ear*
               and then joins those on the perimeter)
               Hello! I had to be persuaded, bullied, coerced
               to take part in this … this adult version of life.
               I have been threatened. Either you participate or you
               fall by the wayside. Well, I have decided now.
               I will participate – however on my own terms.
               I warn you, I am trailing clouds of elementary adolescence.
               Not only have I been handed the typical
               growing-up problems to deal with, which I was
               brought up to expect and I am grateful to my
               parents for that – and to Miriam too, hi, Miriam
               (waves to her on the sidelines) but in addition,
               believe it or not, I am evolving and being resurrected.
               I'll say that again. I am evolving and being resurrected.
               If that means very little to anyone here, that's not my fault.
               This, as you can imagine, accounts for my familiarity
               with suicidal tendencies, with both debilitating depression
               and onsets of both civic and domestic rebellion. I was
               tasered once and I have occasionally self-harmed.
               I assure you, I am not boasting. Until recently I have
               vacillated between being pro-active and utterly inactive.
               No real satisfaction in either case. While I
               experiment with my existence I no longer consider myself
               to be a member of a family – this mostly to protect Al and
               Trish, whom I respect. They've brought me up and
               now I'm on my own. Now I'm facing up to what I call my
               resurrection, to which I assent, even though I barely
               understand it. I realize that for me it's necessary.
               Evidently the modern life is not for me. I also mentioned
               evolution. A teacher in high school introduced me to that.
               We develop, and finally we evolve. That was how he put it.
               Creative spirit takes hold of our inner parts and urges us
               forward to a place of vantage from where we can look

back, with merciful magnanimity on what we
used to call life. In the meantime we grow.
There. That's that.
I believe that's all that was expected of me,
for the time being. Is that right, Trevor?

TREVOR   Thank you, Tim. What can I say! There's more there
than I know what to do with. But that's beside the point.
Will you join us later, please, when we weave all this
into a dramatic whole?

Scene 2

(**Tim**, *seated at a table, in the background quietly conversing
with a stranger; the* **Males** *and* **Females** *in the foreground.*)

TED   They've been at it for an hour now.
Who is that man with him?

LORRAINE   He just walked in. Never knocked, nor introduced himself.

CARL   Trish doesn't know him. Alphonse doesn't know him.

ANNIE   We were told to stay away. Not to interfere.

FRANK   It's my guess he's an acquaintance from Peru.

RITA   A moment ago Tim seemed angry. He got up. Turned away.
Then returned. It's as if that stranger were wanting to
persuade him of something – wanted to make him
do something he didn't want to do.

TED   Complete supposition!
Women can never just look at the facts.

LORRAINE   Don't tell me you think that what's going on there is normal!
A complete stranger walks in, doesn't say boo to anyone,
looks around for Tim, finds him, sits down with him and
harangues him for an hour. And look how he's dressed!

78

CARL	Yeah, when have you last seen someone wear clothes like that? Those jackets went out of fashion when Paganini played the fiddle.
ANNIE	Oh oh! Tim is angry! Is he going to hit him? No, he just pushed him away. There's an element of risk. We may have to interfere.
FRANK	But Alphonse and Patricia are aware of this. You'd think they'd know if Tim was in danger.
RITA	Not necessarily. They don't understand him any more. I have secretly observed how they speak to each other in low voices in his presence, either because they didn't want to disturb him or because they didn't want to hear him.
TED	So do we take it that Tim is out on his own then?
LORRAINE	He has, you might say, turned into a stranger himself. Could happen to anybody.
CARL	What? What? What's that supposed to mean? Anybody could turn into a stranger? That's backwards and you know it. Strangers gradually become familiar.
ANNIE	Lorraine is right. Some turn into strangers and stay that way. I've met one or two, before and after. It's the damndest thing. The thing is, after a while the stranger comes back, returns to the fold, brings gifts, dispenses blessings, chews his food and sleeps at night like a regular punter. At the same time he radiates eternal life.
FRANK	Oh hahahahahahahaaaa! That's so funny! Radiates eternal life! Sweats it out through the pores, I dare say. Let's have more of those!
RITA	Shhh! Keep it down. Tim knows we're listening.

TED   We're <u>not</u> listening! We can't hear a word they say.

LORRAINE   Why not, I wonder. They're not that far away.
            Have you noticed that we can't hear their voices?
            It's as if you could see what they were saying.
            Of course they gesticulate.
            They move their lips, don't they.

CARL   It's as if an invisible wall were
            erected between them and us.

ANNIE   That in itself is a miracle – and true! I say it's true.
            And behind us there are those who are watching us.
            And unknown to them, they too are being watched,
            by benevolent spirits whose hearts they break when they
            behave so ignorantly.

FRANK   Easy on! Not for us to make judgments.

RITA   Oh come on! If not for us then for who! Are you maybe for-
            getting something?

TED   Oh look! Look! They've come to an arrangement.
            They're shaking hands. The stranger, so it appears,
            has made his point. They have arrived at a conclusion.
            Wouldn't you love to know the outcome?

LORRAINE   No, not really. It's not for us to know what those in
            exalted positions think about. It would only confuse us.
            The stranger has gone. Here comes Tim.

CARL   Hello Tim! How's it going?

TIM   (makes as if to walk past them, then returns)
            I'm sorry. I don't mean to be unfriendly.
            What were you saying?

LORRAINE   Oh nothing. We were wondering who that was. The chap in
            the unconventional garb.

TIM   Ah yes! I see what you mean. He was not from here.
            We spoke in Spanish, but please, not so that you couldn't

80

understand. He has no English. We just compared notes, that's all. They have plans for me. Must go.
(exit)

CARL   Plans? For Timothy? What's our Timothy up to?

ANNIE   <u>Our</u> Timothy?
              Are you maybe slipping into a mood of abstraction?
              Our Timothy indeed!

FRANK   Quite right! Our Timothy indeed!
              Does the elephant hobnob with the shriek-owl?
              Do the natives discuss business with the owner of the
              sugar plantation? Can the earthworm divine the esoteric
              purpose of a rocket to Pluto?

RITA   Does a breeze from the East bring news of the earth's veloc-
              ity through space?

TED   Hey, this is fun. Still, it niggles.
              'They have plans for me.'
              What sort of plans? And who are they?
              I'm not looking for answers, don't get me wrong.

LORRAINE   No, I know, you are merely heightening the sense of
              expectation. Nothing wrong with that.
              Although I question your timing.

TREVOR   (*enters*)
              Good! Enough! Too much already. Let's wrap it up.
              One of the cameras ran out of film, but not to worry.
              Time for lunch. Back at two-thirty, please, if you can
              at all manage it. And if you stuff yourselves you'll be
              no good to anyone. And no alcohol before sundown,
              Frank, or you'll be the only one who thinks he's clever.

(all leave stage, empty except for the table and two chairs,
in silence for one minute)

———

Scene 3

(**Trevor**, **Trish**, **Alphonse**, **Miriam**)

TREVOR   Are you sure you want me to be part of this?
Sometimes I feel that the personal affairs of my actors
should not be allowed to concern me. We do, after all,
have a professional task ahead of us.

MIRIAM   Which is what, Trevor?

TREVOR   Why, nothing more nor less than to encourage
human beings in their human being and humanity;
to remind them of their communality, to lead them
to the joy of human-natural affection, to allow them to …

ALPHONSE   Enough already! Trevor, the less said <u>about</u> that the better.
You are liable to turn into an idealist and idealism is the
scourge of life.

TRISH   By the way, Trevor, you are wearing your jacket inside out.
It looks most peculiar.

TREVOR   Oh dear! I was in a rush. (*he corrects that*)
But you must tell me now what this is about. Don't forget,
we have a practice session this afternoon.

ALPHONSE   It's about Tim, Trevor.

TREVOR   Yes. I see what you mean. What is he up to?
What is going on with him? He had a visitor this morning.
Most peculiar-looking chap. Foreigner, by the looks of him.
And why is Tim not here with us right now?

TRISH   A delicate matter, Trevor. In Peru Tim became involved
with a group of people who call themselves anarchists.
He has always refused to talk about it. Says it would only
cause us anxiety.

TREVOR   Do those people call themselves anarchists or do outsiders
call them that?

ALPHONSE   Very good, Trevor. You've put you finger on it.
           Neither they themselves nor Trevor call themselves
           anarchists. It seems they do not call themselves
           anything in particular at all. As a consequence
           the authorities have taken a dim view of them.

MIRIAM   They call them anarchists because they cannot find a
           political category for them.

ALPHONSE   As for us, who are not much smarter, we want to see
           if we can somehow transform our own anxiety
           into a common understanding. Otherwise, you see,
           Miriam worries, I worry, Patricia worries, and all in our
           own separate ways, the common denominator of which
           is ignorance. We have brought Tim up,
           the three of us, really – as you know, Miriam has
           always been a caring third parent for Tim and he
           appreciated that – we have raised him to the stage
           where he began to think and feel for himself and now
           we have to trust that he has what it takes to make his
           own mistakes and to learn from them. That's readily said
           but difficult to put into practice.

TREVOR   But look here, you must have some notion of
           what's in his mind. At least during the
           early stages of his involvement with that group of –
           whatever they are – he must have talked to you about it.

TRISH   Well, he did, Trevor, of course. He expressed his
           dissatisfaction, his anger, his impatience with the world,
           with society, with the lack of honesty and loyalty and
           nobility in his environment. Typical teenage growing-pains,
           we decided and looked the other way. Then he spoke
           no more about it. He internalized it, I dare say.
           He became a stranger to us.

ALPHONSE   That's a bit unfair, Trish, sorry, I have to correct that.

No, not correct it, but explain how I see it.
Only to the extent that we still held on to him did he
seem to become strange. And surely that's to be expected.
I never told you this, Trish, but once I actually said to him:
Tim, don't feel you have to discuss everything with your
parents. We don't want to hold you back. You are
bound to want to think about human existence in your
own way. He thanked me for that.

TRISH That's hard for a mother, isn't it, Miriam.

MIRIAM Well, with two of us – let's be honest – it's only
half the worry. Some mothers are alone with their
concerns for their sons. Especially if the husband is a dud.

TIM (enters) Oh, pardon me. I don't want to interrupt.
I must have left my phone in here. There it is, look.
I'll just retrieve it and be gone.

ALPHONSE Tim!

TIM Yes, father?

ALPHONSE Would you stay with us for a few minutes?
Have you the time?

TIM Yes, of course. I'll make time. Let me make a call
and I'll be back shortly. (leaves)

MIRIAM Is this a good idea, Alphonse? Did we not want to …

ALPHONSE I'm suggesting a change of plans, I know.
But let's face it, we're talking about our son.
So why can't we speak to him in person –
about what worries us? Wait till you see, it will
be alright. Trish?

TRISH Why shouldn't it be alright. Especially with Trevor here.
Please, Trevor, if we may use your presence here as a
reminder of what communication is all about.

84

TREVOR   I'll be entirely guided by your wishes.

TIM   (*enters*) Here I am. I've even brought my own chair.
            Am I not the model of consideration?
            But now I have to say, you all look rather apprehensive.
            Are you quite sure you want me to be part of this?
            How about if I sit here, beside you, Alphonse.
            Is that alright? Not too close, not too far. Just the right dis-
            tance for a father-son relationship.

ALPHONSE   Tim! What has come over you?
            You are not your customary taciturn self.

TIM   Me? Taciturn? Please! Oh, I see what you mean.
            Yes, well, I can explain that. You wonder why I am
            cheerful? I have had good news. From Lima.
            My best friend has been freed. From jail.
            This is such a good sign, for all of us. Perhaps we will be
            left alone for a while now. I'm sorry, but I cannot sit
            while I talk about this. It is such good news.

TRISH   Of course we know nothing about your friends, Tim,
            you are aware of that, are you not. We are happy for you,
            and for your friend, but why was he incarcerated?

TIM   Oh, they might have picked any one of us.
            We are perfectly respectful to the authorities, by the way.
            We make no trouble. We cause no disturbance,
            neither civic nor political.

TREVOR   Surely you do something?

TIM   Yes, we stand peacefully at street corners, in parks, on
            islands in the middle of busy traffic,
            and we wish everyone well.

MIRIAM   You wish everyone well?

TIM   Yes, we have decided it's the very best we can do.
            If we do more, we are passing judgment,

85

which we consider to be wrong.
Wishing everyone well, everyone in our vicinity,
that, for us, is a very important, and effective,
personal occupation. It is also an individual contribution,
because each one does it in his or her own way –
all inwardly of course, where the true reality has its seat
and from where it stems. Some do it joyfully, some do it
lovingly, others again do it by means of cheerful suffering.
Sounds unusual, doesn't it. We do discuss it at length.

TREVOR   You say this is effective, Tim. How can it be effective?
You don't choose to speak to anyone? You stand still?

TIM   We do. We stand perfectly still. Inwardly, however,
we are very active. You must imagine that
wherever we stand we are bound to be influenced
by what goes on around us, by the various manifestations
of modern anxiety. We are bombarded, you might say,
by the fear and trembling, by the hidden terrors, the
concealed guilt and shame, of those in our immediate
surroundings and instead of shutting ourselves
off from this influence, we respond to it.

TREVOR   That's the damndest thing I've ever heard.

TRISH   So you stand there empty-handed and you suffer the modern
plague to come onto you.

TIM   And that already does good. We all make a point of
understanding how spirit works,
how creative suffering overcomes.

ALPHONSE What sort of thing would you mostly be dealing with,
while you stand there?
I mean in yourselves.

TIM   Oh, everything from just plain fatigue and
impatience to anger and ill will.

High spirits and low spirits.
It's a full time job, believe me. Many want to join us,
few can persevere. I often have to overcome
disgust and lethargy.

TRISH   And if someone addresses you?

TIM   Then, of course, we have what we call the
golden opportunity. The ready inward response leaps
out into the light of day. At times people are quite
astonished by what they get. Usually by the time someone
talks to us we have good will stored up, you see.

TREVOR   So why was your friend pulled in? Does that happen often?

TIM   No it doesn't. The authorities wanted to know what we were
up to. Luckily they picked on my friend who is
super-secure in his work and very personable.
You know, no self-justification, no disrespect – so I
dare say his explanations satisfied them. Needless to say
we were all concerned, because you never know. You don't
dare blame people. What, after all, can they know?
There are only about fifty of us, so far. And not just in Peru.
It's so easy to keep in touch, thanks to the internet.

ALPHONSE So you've really come to the conclusion that …

TIM   For now, yes. I suppose it's sad, once you realize that
nowadays very little else <u>can</u> work.
Every gesture that we can imagine can be turned
against the human being within us. There's a
raging spirit on the go … anti-reason; purely cold criticism
devoid of all allegiance to the truth … oh it's
monstrous once you stand face to face with it
and all the light goes out. We're all young, you see, and
willing to try anything. Which is why we have a handle on
the ruthless truth, no holds barred, just absolute
perfection. And all in the name of the spirit that is love.

TRISH	You sort of advance one little step at a time, don't you.
TIM	Yes, without programs, without mantras, without the least hope or expectation of recognition or popular success.
MIRIAM	Each of you totally on his own – I must admit it sounds frightening. Like free-climbing up El Cap. All I can say is I'm glad someone is doing this – because – I have a hunch it absolutely needs to be done. And eventually will it be … what? … accomplished?
TIM	I think so, Miriam. We are doing this for many. And they don't need to know that we're doing it. Also we're staying sane this way. Look, I need to head on now. I hope you won't worry about me. I understand how what I'm doing is worth-while. Will you be able to keep that in mind?
TRISH	Yes Tim. Do get in touch now and again.
TIM	(*on his way out*) Thank you for including me in your deliberations.
MIRIAM and ALPHONSE	
	Thanks for joining us, Tim.

(Tim leaves)

TRISH	Oh dear – so cold – so noble!
MIRIAM	Emotions are dead – long live emotion.

Scene 4

(**Trevor, Miriam, Trish** *and* **Alphonse**)

TREVOR	Do you recall, Miriam – of course you do – all those years ago, when you gave your baby up for adoption?
MIRIAM	Well, technically, I offered my baby to Alphonse and Patricia. Happily they accepted. Because look at the result!

88

TREVOR	Indeed! Imagine if instead of three parents he'd had five or six! I dare say your concern for him is eased somewhat now?
TRISH	It is, Trevor. Of course. I find his degree of understanding phenomenal. This notion of his – the creative domain within – well, at that age I was still trying to, quote: 'find myself'. He and his friends are taking on the modern spirit.
ALPHONSE	I personally would always have expected someone who is wise from within to dedicate his energies to some art, and to art-works – and to avoid the – what – the open field, but these chaps are choosing to come face to face with the raw population. I wonder …
TRISH	Are you thinking what I'm thinking?
ALPHONSE	Very likely, Patricia. What if we were to explore that dilemma, that contradiction, playfully and dramatically? We would certainly require our usual chorus.
TREVOR	Would we be able to explain to them what's at stake? Don't forget, they weren't with us while Tim told us what he does.
ALPHONSE	Surely it's best if they don't know.
TREVOR	Ah, I see what you mean! Yes! I'm stupid. Why not, then? I've asked them to be ready for work at two o'clock.
TRISH	The thing, then, is to avoid all direct mention of what Tim was talking about while the four of us – I take it you want to be part of this, Trevor – yes – good! – while the four of us come as close as we can to building and shaping the symbolic action of what Tim meant. Not that different from what we've done before, but perhaps with the added insistence on spontaneity.

TREVOR   So we respond from within to what Ted and Lorraine
            and the others, in their comparative ignorance,
            confront us with. I will have to give them some indication.

TRISH   The bare bones, Trevor.

TREVOR   Agreed. I eat lunch with my good wife and children today.
            You will suit yourselves and we'll meet up at two?

ALPHONSE   That's fine, Trevor.

(they depart severally)

———————

Act V

Scene 1

(first **Trevor,** *then* **Alphonse, Trish, Miriam,** *the* **Males** *and the* **Females;** *later* **Vivian** *and* **Uncle Werner)**

TREVOR Right, folks, before we start this fifth act, a little lecture. You know how all along we have tried to avoid the so-called voyeurism of the modern drama. We find it distasteful, disgusting and downright indigestible. It has dawned on us that the modern audience has in turns been cajoled and seduced into the bad habit of hugging its privacy – its privation, we might call it – while detaching itself as completely as possible from the public spectacle. We are no longer willing to take these sneaky peeks through a keyhole at what is being presented to us as our own guilty secret. No one can indulge in that with impunity. Eventually the bottom drops out of our humanity. The contemporary drama, in comparison and contrast to the modern variety, leaves the audience in peace, both during and after the art-experience. No more sexy seductions. No more self-indulgence. Those who insist on that can run themselves down in the privacy of their own homes. They get plenty of help from the mass-media. Of course I wouldn't say this so blatantly outside these four walls. Besides, no one can switch over just like that from the modern decadence to a contemporary appreciation of an art-work; so the accent, for a while, will be on what I think of as friendly persuasion. As a consequence, in this fifth act, we distinguish, for the duration, between those in the know and those not in the know, in other words between, on one side, Trish, Alphonse and Miriam, then Vivian and Uncle Werner later of course, and on the other side you six, our Males and Females, as you choose to call yourselves. Alphonse, would you please begin?

ALPHONSE   Right from the start I've been in preparation for this.
            I see myself as a criminal who has never faced up to the
            truth about himself.

TRISH   Alphonse! Is that really the right note for a good start?
            Shouldn't we ...

ALPHONSE   No! Please! You make your contribution, I make mine.
            I have barely started and you interrupt me. The criminal
            on one side, I say, and the hypocrite on the other.
            The two are in cahoots. What they come up with I call
            the modern mix. Then of course, at the same time –
            contemporaneously, if you don't mind long words –
            there's the me I myself don't see and that I myself
            cannot see. I call that the human being which I am: the
            'I am that I am'. The person. The one who comes out of
            hiding when I speak to you lot, as I do at the present.
            Do you see what I mean?

LORRAINE   I ask myself why would anyone be interested in this,
            Alphonse. Just be yourself. Tell us a joke, begin with that.
            Or am I missing the point here?

MIRIAM   Alphonse is obviously trying to set the stage. It's up to
            each one of us either to join him on that stage or to set our
            own example.

TED   Or to walk away, I take it.

TRISH   No! You take it wrong. No one who is anyone can walk
            away. As soon as we make the least attempt even to turn
            away, the clouds come down, the thunder speaks, the light-
            ning strikes.

TED   Oh pardonnez-moi! Tsk, tsk. I'm so ignorant.

LORRAINE   Well you are. I knew right away what Miriam meant.

ANNIE   Yesterday evening I saw God dancing as a murmuration
            of starlings.

92

RITA   At the hairdresser's this morning a woman I'd never seen
           before offered me her holiday home in Spain for a week.

TREVOR   (*enters*) This is going well. Keep it up. (*exits*)

ALPHONSE   From within my soul I offer the truth to the world.

THE CHORUS   (*cheerful laughter!*)

ALPHONSE   Thank you. And ever alert to such a cheerful response
           from our beloved chorus, I have brought these bags of
           sweets. Here. Catch. What I mean is, the way our
           high-rise buildings scrape the sky and equally the way
           hundreds of rockets break <u>through</u> the sky on their way to
           extra-terrestrial destinations, this causes me neither
           heart-ache nor mind-set but I view it as an aspect of the
           modern dream.

TRISH   You wish it well?

ALPHONSE   I do indeed.

CARL   Good boy, Alphonse. Good man! Hats off, gentlemen!

ANNIE   You mean Ladies and Gentlemen, I take it.

CARL   Oh that. Yes, surely. I'm still trying to figure out
           what this lot is really on about. They're up to something,
           that's clear. Frank, you are keeping quiet. Have you any
           idea what they're up to?

FRANK   I really don't see how it's our business to figure that out.
           Personally I think they're digging holes for themselves,
           but then maybe they're just looking for solid rock
           to build on.

MIRIAM   The question I feel constrained to ask is: Whence springs
           a woman's wisdom? It seems to me at times – and I fear
           it may be the case – that we know it when we have it but
           when we have it not we don't know how to acquire it. I
           would welcome input from any source.

93

LORRAINE	I get it! I think I get it! We are half-consciously involved here in a sort of musical composition. Annie, what say you? When I pay close attention to what must surely come next I merely have to look to myself with an eye to virtue itself and my wildest dreams no longer play a role but they – how shall I put it – help me out here, Annie – they are condensed as a fine mist and settle out upon the atmospheric environment. Wild dreams, in other words, transpire and a new world rises from the art of the heart. How quaint!
ANNIE	You seem to be dead set upon making a fool of yourself.
TRISH	Oh come along, Annie. Credit where credit is due. Lorraine has stepped out of character to good purpose. I dearly wish we might all rise to that occasion betimes. Lorraine, try again, do. Spread your sail to the fantasy of the moment.
ANNIE	God help us!
LORRAINE	Very well, I just will. Though I won't guarantee a thing. (uncomfortable *pause*)
TRISH	What? No use?
LORRAINE	Oh yes. Sorry. I forgot to say it out loud.
MIRIAM	Oh you must communicate, dear.
ANNIE	They are laying a trap for you, stupid.
MIRIAM	Not at all. How dare you say such a thing! Lorraine! Make her wrong!
LORRAINE	Alright. I will. With the heart of a lion I stride forth onto the quicksilver meadow of my soul – I call for my unicorn steed, mount up and – (pause) damn! The thing won't move. What am I doing wrong, Trish? Help me!

TRISH	You must lean more lovingly into the wind, dear.
LORRAINE	All I can see now is hummingbirds, white sheets flapping on the line, an immensity of space all around, waiting to be filled – to be made liveable. And a dove. A white, ringed dove.
ANNIE	Wring its neck, dear, and roast it for your supper.
LORRAINE	Well, how did I do? Was I wise?
MIRIAM	I believe we'd do well to appreciate your courage, Lorraine. It's perfectly true that not all of us were on your side while you were struggling but you made it through, yes you did. Congratulations! Now make use of what you've learned, in the days to come. Practice is of the essence.
ANNIE	What? What has she learned? Excuse me, but I would like to know.
ALPHONSE	You will have to wait for another opportunity, Annie. You will get it. But stay alert.
TREVOR	(enters) The fact that this dramatic enterprise remains apparently unstructured is bound to upset the aficionados, whereupon, I dare say, you, Alphonse, will have your bags of sweets ready.
ALPHONSE	Right you are, Trevor. Now leave us to it please. We are not out of the doldrums yet. I mean as a group. And it's the group that counts.
TREVOR	Fair enough. (exit)
FRANK	I still think you are all – you lot, I mean – digging holes for yourselves. I just can't see it leading anywhere. I've been watching and watching. Hoping for a sign. Trembling on the cusp of despair. I'm joking, of course, I can't take it that seriously, except that I'd like to take part.

95

However don't I have to be able to conceive the overall purpose first, the general goal, quite independently of the particular detours? (*pause*) Well, don't I?

ALPHONSE You smiled there, Frank, like an American who has just arrived from his dentist's appointment wearing his new set of sparklers. You are ill at ease. You place too much emphasis on appearances. On <u>signs</u> of the truth. How telling, that you should speak up just when we have hit rock bottom. We start building now. Why not join us, regardless of the how, what, why, when and where? This is when we take advantage of the unforeseeable. Don't look so embarrassed. Look happy. That will make you happy.

MIRIAM What a relief, eh? Who was afraid we might not make it? Who? Own up now, come along.

TREVOR (*enters*) Pardon me, two visitors hoping to be allowed to join you. They have <u>my</u> permission.

TRISH Oh look! Uncle Werner and Vivian! Welcome! Yes. Join us, please. We are just on the upswing of an experimental act. I dare say the strain is telling. Is Galina with you?

VIVIAN Galina has died. (*pause*) No, hang on! She lost weight, never courage. She dwindled and could not even speak in the end. We were with her during her last hour. She wished you all well and assured you that she would soon see us all again, 'towards the end of her resurrection'. Those are her words, even as I give them to you and I don't apologize for them.

ALPHONSE Evidently her death was nothing final?

UNCLE W. Bless you, Alphonse, for understanding. There was nothing wrong with her health. As for her wellbeing,

she evidently found herself within a profound
learning-situation.

TED What's this now, when someone dies,
That's the end, he doesn't rise,
And if he does, it's on the other side.

LORRAINE All my life I've looked far and wide
For some excuse, some prejudice
That makes my life less hit or miss.

CARL You say she died and yet she lives?
That's nonsense, isn't it? What gives?
I'd want to feel her pulse in the end.

ANNIE We've had this guff for two millennia now.
We're tired of supernatural gods
Of worm-eaten peas in gorgeous pods.

FRANK Who is it dies and lives again
Within our memory and our soul?
I've heard it said: that makes us whole.

RITA Of course we might some day find out
There's something to be said for living
As though we're dead to the old world –
I'll have to think about that.

VIVIAN Oh well done, you lot! You'd swear
Some thought had got into them there.

UNCLE W. Vivian! I've never known you to be disrespectful.

VIVIAN Was I? Oh dear! I am sorry. It's the rhyme, you know.
Causes a person to become superficial and self-centred.

UNCLE W. So what are you all up to? You seem to be
enjoying yourselves.

TREVOR *(who has been standing by)*
They have not been wasting their time, though it

97

might have seemed like it to you, had you been
here earlier. They have traced the creative process
from its very inception to where we have it now,
and your arrival, you two, plus your announcement
of Galina's death, has marked for us our own arrival
in the here and now. It sounds so complicated because
it's so very simple. 'The golden opportunity'
Tim called it a short while ago.

VIVIAN   Tim?

TREVOR   Yes, Tim has been and gone again. He taught us a
           great thing. What would you call it, Patricia, if you had to
           put a name to what he taught us?

TRISH   Oh, the drama of truth, perhaps. It appears that youth
           is no longer content with our modern habit of skipping
           along the surface and calling it culture and civilization.
           The young are persuaded of the soundness of their human
           nature and will no longer allow anyone to meddle with it.

VIVIAN   But that is great news! It's a thing I have long maintained.

UNCLE W.   And shall we not anticipate that Galina will eventually
           point us in that same direction? Will she not figure as the
           feminine equivalent to what I believe you have described
           as Tim's dramatic breakthrough? If only I had been there
           to witness it.

ALPHONSE   It happened to him in Lima, Peru, and he
           cooperated, you see. Then it turned into a
           communal thing. It seems there are many now
           who are becoming familiar with the operation
           of their soul. Not that easy to describe.

TED   Possibly not worth describing at all because it's nonsense.

CARL   It's not nonsense, it's worse than nonsense, it's the
           attempt to undermine all our values, the values we've

98

fought for these past centuries and finally we can say we reach for the stars and what happens? (*pause*)

UNCLE W.   Well, alright, tell us what happens.

CARL   All you have to do is look around. World-wide insecurity. Absurd attempts to resurrect the nation state.

FRANK   This plague of unwillingness to realize that anxiety is the cause of all sicknesses and diseases, and it's no wonder, because the magicians and the sorcerers have invested their survival in the concerted attempt to base continued existence on the fruits of materialism: the absurdity of eternal economic growth.

LORRAINE   Calm down! Calm down! How I hate male hysteria! Besides, you miss the point entirely.

TREVOR   I think you should …

LORRAINE   You keep quiet and let me speak. You always miss the point. The cold facts indicate that whenever the spook of metaphysics raises its hoary head we're in for a time of the worst darkness and confusion.

ANNIE   That's right! She's right! Let her speak! It's high time the females of the world linked arms and marched. You guys forever talk overtop of us. This burying of the head in the sand will no longer be tolerated.

TREVOR   Come along now, you're not here to make a nuisance of yourselves. You're supposed to …

RITA   (*pushing Trevor aside*)
What makes you think you have the right to tell us what to do? Your time is up.
Look at that lot in the corner there!
(*pointing at Alphonse, Trish and Miriam who have retreated*)
They sneer at us, you can see the contempt in their eyes,

99

to them we're consumers, canon-fodder, justifications
for over-production, all they're worried about is that
their blessed living-standard should rise and rise and rise –
how high can it rise anyway? And what's the point
when quality goes down the tubes?

TED   (*pushing her out of his way*) You shut up now, big-mouth.

LORRAINE   (*pushing him out of her way*) No, you shut up!
             How dare you push her out of the way!

VIVIAN   Trevor, do something.

LORRAINE   It's show-down time, folks. Time for the male to get his
             come-uppance. Let's just gang up on them, that frightens
             them, and then the 'coup de grace'. You wouldn't hit a
             woman, would you? (*Lorraine and Ted continue to fight*)
             Don't forget, the idea is to get them under, us on top.
             It's high time.

TREVOR   That's enough now! Stop!

RITA   (*strikes him down*) You don't count just now.
             Lie there and look at the world from below for a while.

VIVIAN   How dare you! Are you totally mad?

RITA   You bet, sunshine. This is madness! We're mad alright!
             Mad!

FRANK   (*strikes her down from behind*)
             There you go. I didn't think I'd ever get myself
             to do that, but actually it felt great.
             It's the last hurdle to take. Who do they think they are,
             fucking females. And we used to try to be nice to them.
             For form's sake. Those days are over, right mate?

CARL   You bet. Days of wine and roses. Chivalry!
             Ladies and gentlemen! It's the war of the sexes
             and only one outcome is possible.

ANNIE   (*who has rushed off for a knife, stabs him from behind*)
Right you are. Here's your outcome.
Didn't think that would happen, did you.
Bastard. Lousy bastard. Oh what a treat!
How I've looked forward to this!
No more conscience!
To hell with morality!
Down with religion!

FRANK   (*disappears to get a gun;* **Annie** *in the opposite direction, to get a gun: both return and shoot each other; one report is heard*)

ANNIE and FRANK
Take that!
(*both fall down dead*)

LORRAINE and TED
[*they are obviously fatigued but still able, in the end, to strangle each other; this takes half a minute, while* **Alphonse, Trish, Miriam, Vivian** *and* **Uncle Werner** *watch in horror. In the end, six bodies (the* **Chorus**) *lie dead; there is a long pause –*]

GALINA   (*enters*)
Your suffering has torn at my heartstrings.
How long must this strife have festered,
like an open wound! They, like ourselves,
are dear to the creator. In the end they cannot
help themselves, they must do as they are driven.
We are all driven at times but we have
laid in the insurance of human-natural affection
and of common kindliness. There is one who
weeps for the human race, for mankind at the
brink of self-destruction. We cannot
manage without him. This I have learned,
on both sides of death – of death as the

challenge and death as the liberator.
What these have illustrated, over the past two
millennia, may benefit us as a show of consequences,
of what happens when we espouse sacrifice
instead of mercy.
It falls to me to raise them from their torpor.
Some will prosper, some will fail.
(*She touches each one in turn on the head; they come to
their senses and rise to their feet. Trevor gets up unaided.*)

TREVOR   That was the damndest outbreak of sheer evil.

GALINA   I can imagine. I felt it, where I was, by myself, meditating.
All he same, I had to wait, before I came,
until I knew it was over. The human drama has to
take its course; we can but take care of ourselves
and of one another while the modern performance
draws to its end.

TREVOR   Come now, the six of you, you've done well.
You need to rest from your labours.
No harm done, I hope, on account of the
rough and tumble?

LORRAINE   Oh you know us, we enjoy a thorough slog through the
elemental terrain. Come along, girls, we'll prepare
some refreshments. Lads, you too.
Won't you give us a hand?

TED   Surely. Carl, you willing? Frank?

FRANK   I'm going home. I've had quite enough of this carry-on.

LORRAINE   Oh oh! We've lost one. Never mind. Bound to happen.

––––––––––

Scene 2

TREVOR   Well, it looks like we're near the end – no bones broken.
                You probably wonder why I stayed down so long,
                after Rita smacked me. I couldn't have got up. I tried.
                It was like a paralysis. At the same time
                the coward in me said: Stay out of the way and you
                won't get hurt.

ALPHONSE   Where did they get the weapons? The knives and the guns?

UNCLE W.   Human ingenuity, Alphonse. Weapons of destruction
                become more sophisticated until the destruction is complete.

GALINA   Or until the construction begins, surely.

VIVIAN   How are you now, Galina? You appeared thoroughly
                distraught when you arrived.

GALINA   I was sleepwalking, Vivian. That's how it felt. When I
                opened my mouth, words came out. I was a voice.
                I can imagine that your players are used to that, Trevor,
                but it took me by surprise. And it was true what I said.
                I was sitting comfortably in my apartment, reading a book,
                when I became progressively more anxious.
                Suddenly I behaved like a robot.
                I quietly put my book down, walked over here
                and behaved the way you saw.

TREVOR   You see that? There are those who make light of the acting
                profession.

TRISH   Also there are those, I suppose, who just plain don't know
                how to play a personal role and they go to a theatre and let
                others do it for them.

MIRIAM   Oh, haha, I fit into that category. I think the link in me is
                missing that would join me to the rest of humanity.
                So I have to pretend. It's alright, you know.
                Don't feel sorry for me.

103

TREVOR   Here, we're forgetting about the chorus.
It's only right that we should look in on them for a
few minutes. Did I hear Lorraine say they would …
                  (*on hold*)

———

Scene 3

(*Lorraine, Annie* and *Rita; Ted* and *Frank;* then *Tim*,
in the canteen or kitchen)

LORRAINE   I'm bushed! Bloody hell, what came over us!
I could have sworn you guys were out for my blood.
I was defending myself, your honour,
I'll swear to that on a bible.

TED   It happens, let's not pretend otherwise.
There's not enough milk! No, wait, here's another bottle.
It happens. Mind you, that time it happened a bit
too quick for my liking. When hatred gets into a person
the world shrinks down to a pin prick.

ANNIE   It was too much for Carl. We'll not see Carl again.
I'm sorry about that. I liked Carl. You never know, do you,
what's inside a person until the chips are down.

FRANK   Carl has come to grief and there's no doubt about that.
Here, those biscuits are still fresh, what a surprise!
Let's set everything up on the big table and then
we'll call them in.

RITA   I was mad. Stark raving mad. It was Vivian that set me off.
Under ordinary circumstances I have the greatest
respect for that man. Somebody hit me over the head from
behind. Just in time too. Was that you, Frank?
I would have gone for Vivian. Wow, what a headline:
Murder on the stage.

FRANK   I hit somebody. It might have been you. I was in a frenzy. Gosh, the old saying is true, isn't it: While you're in a frenzy you're not responsible, but you're responsible for being in a frenzy. Usually people understand that long afterwards.

ANNIE   Like in the penitentiary. No, never mind, we don't need serviettes. We don't need a tablecloth either. You make me nervous, Rita. You should get married. Be a housewife. It's a noble calling.

LORRAINE You smacked Trevor, Rita. What possessed you? No, that's not butter. Use proper butter. And slice up more Veda. They're bound to be hungry.

RITA   There again, you see, it wasn't me who hit him but the devil in me. I blame the devil. We should always blame the devil, then no one has to be tried and judged. So much simpler.

TED   But why Trevor? He's one of us, isn't he?

LORRAINE Oh Ted! For goodness' sake! One of us! What does that ever mean when the chaos breaks out?

TED   Well, nobody went for Vivian, or Trish, or that lot. Why was that? But obviously Rita thought Trevor was fair game.

ANNIE   I'm sure thought did not come into it, Ted. All the same, you do have a point. Doesn't he, Lorraine. We went for each other, including Trevor. They just watched. Probably they were horrified. Must ask them. Maybe they understand. Ah! Look who's here! Hello Tim! Are you sneaking in through the kitchen?

TIM   I missed my flight. Drones in the sky. Don't let me interrupt. This was the only door that was open. Where is everybody?

105

LORRAINE	Oh they'll all be in here in a minute. Sit down, have a sandwich. Steal a march on the gods.
TIM	Thanks very much, Lorraine. It must be close to quitting-time, am I right? I suppose you'll all be wanting to talk shop.
FRANK	Oh no, please! I'm done for today. Relaxation, leisure and ease, that's the order for the rest of the day.
ANNIE	I think we've all had just about enough drama for one day. Tim, will you light the big candle? It always gets lit when we're packing up. That's the sign for: No more analysis!
	(Tim lights the candle)
RITA	I think we're ready. Will I call them in?
LORRAINE	Do. I've been looking forward to this. Wait till they see you sitting here munching your sandwich, Tim.
RITA	*(leaves to call **Trish**, **Alphonse**, **Miriam**, **Galina**, **Vivian** and **Uncle Werner**, who enter and make a fuss over **Tim**)*

Scene 4

(*Trevor, Galena and Tim*)

TREVOR	We have arrived at the point of our play Where nothing remains to be said except: The purpose of our human wisdom will always be To align ourselves with merciful good spirit In all our works and in all our communality, For it is the love we have for one another that Makes us accessible to universal good being.
GALINA	Men, women and children live on earth for that One reason that they shall find their satisfaction Not among the stars nor underground where

Fools avoid the unfathomable care of the creator
And where strife forever vies with cupidity –
But in cheerful acceptance of divine genius
As it guides our varied personality on earth,
And as it shares in our daily realization of
What it means to live well and meaningfully.

TIM The last word belongs to me because I'm young
And obedient to the promptings of good spirit
Within, where all that is required of us nowadays
To counteract the destructive influences of evil
Is beautifully revealed and truthfully shaped.
We who are young today seek within ourselves
The mature wisdom that has always been our
Birthright, for within us it presses and agitates,
That we might lay down our life for one another:
Not the life that allows us to survive to old age
But eternal life, that is joy and supreme satisfaction;
Eternal life that is appreciation of each new day,
The very life that means human-natural affection
For the greatness of what is childlike and small.
To that end too we respect those among us
Who have learned how to make human existence
Comfortable, pleasurable and convenient,
For at ease, not anxiously, we achieve our goals –
And to that same end we honour those among us
To whom it is given to interpret the signals and
To reveal the secrets pertinent to the present day.
   "This am I,"
Says the One who inhabits the world we love.

———————

Epilogue

(two Ladies)

LADY 1   That took a long time. I came here wanting to be
            entertained. Instead something else happened and I'll be
            darned if I know what it is. What, in your opinion,
            have you gained from this so-called art-experience?

LADY 2   It's far too early to talk about that. Right now I feel
            grouchy. Downcast. Joyless, really. I wish I hadn't come
            and I wish I weren't here. It's as if I'd been brought
            face to face with myself and I don't like what I see.

LADY 1   Usually what I do when I feel like that is I ask for joy.
            I haven't done that yet.

LADY 2   So don't just talk about it. Do it. Ask. I'll help you.
            Let's both ask. There must be some good reason
            why we're not alone but in each other's company.
            We're almost friends, after all, although that shouldn't
            make any difference one way or the other.

LADY 1   I want to be joyful now. Cheerful and joyful.
            And I want that for you too, by the way.
            I've been for too long stuck in my own individuality.

LADY 2   It's great, that at our age we're both aware of the
            life-riches available to us for the asking. Were you
            brought up to know that?

LADY 1   Not really. I was brought up to believe that joy depended on
            my getting things. As a consequence joy was a periodic ac-
            cident, and at that only a facsimile. When I got married, my
            husband taught me different. I wish he were still around.
            Sometimes I wish that. Mostly I understand that
            his time was up.

LADY 2   I learned about joy from books. The Gospel of John,
            especially. Oh how I poured over that text! Even as a child

I wanted to know why so many people were so sad.
Especially, why were they so constricted in such dire
circumstances and to them there seemed to be no way out.
I myself soon knew of a way out and when I
told them about it they looked at me with complete
lack of understanding.

LADY 1   Yes, what a boon is understanding! To understand why
we're around. To understand that we're in good hands.

LADY 2   The thing is, you can't *make* anyone understand.
That used to make me ever so sad. All you can do is
set your example.

LADY 1   Well, don't call it: 'all you can do'. It's a great deal,
when you do that. It's a million ways of behaving.
Of responding. Of being creative, and helpful, and
generally ready to leap into the breach.
Knowing that keeps me on my toes.

LADY 2   Yes of course. I sometimes make degenerative remarks.
Oh dear, poor me, are the times not terrible, am I not
badly done by!

LADY 1   Yes, that's a great way of bringing on that general
malaise in which we get stuck then,
so that all we can do is complain and
lower the tone in particular. Ha! What a laugh!

LADY 2   And have you not noticed how careful we have to be
so that when we actually do feel miserable
we don't take it out on those around us?

LADY 1   Yes, or bury it inside ourselves as though it didn't exist –
because we're afraid others will notice?

LADY 2   Ah, there now, you've put your finger on the value of
creativity. The ability to step into god so as to leave the
devil behind. That's the trick, isn't it?

109

LADY 1   It is. Let's go home now. We've done what we can here.
                                (Both leave)

————————————

* * * * *